MEMOIR

OF

COL. BENJAMIN TALLMADGE,

𝔓𝔯𝔢𝔭𝔞𝔯𝔢𝔡 𝔟𝔶 𝔥𝔦𝔪𝔰𝔢𝔩𝔣, 𝔞𝔱 𝔱𝔥𝔢 ℜ𝔢𝔮𝔲𝔢𝔰𝔱 𝔬𝔣 𝔥𝔦𝔰 ℭ𝔥𝔦𝔩𝔡𝔯𝔢𝔫.

New York:

THOMAS HOLMAN, BOOK AND JOB PRINTER, CORNER OF CENTRE AND WHITE STREETS.

1858.

1836
80

Benj.ⁿ Tallmadge

FROM A PENCIL SKETCH BY COL. TRUMBULL

PREFACE.

THE following Memoir of Colonel BENJAMIN TALL-
MADGE was prepared by himself, at the request of his
children, and for their gratification. It is confined,
principally, to those incidents of the Revolutionary
War with which he was more immediately connected,
and therefore becomes the more interesting to his
descendants and family friends.

For their convenience, and for the additional purpose of contributing to the authenticity of our Revolutionary History, I determined to publish this Memoir;
and, as it terminates with the close of the Revolutionary struggle, I have added a brief sketch of his subsequent life.

As a frontispiece, I have placed an engraved copy
of a pencil sketch of my father, made by Colonel
JOHN TRUMBULL, soon after the close of the Revolutionary War, and which he presented to me, in frame,
a few years before that venerated patriot's death.

I need not say how much I appreciate his kindness,
in furnishing me with so spirited a sketch of my ven-

erable ancestor, as well as the pride that is awakened and gratified, by receiving it from one of the Aids of WASHINGTON, and the companion-in-arms of my father.

F. A. TALLMADGE.

New York, November 16*th,* 1858.

MEMOIR.

The subject of this memoir was born at Brookhaven, on Long Island, in Suffolk county, State of New York, on the 25th of February, 1754. His father, the Rev. Benjamin Tallmadge, was the settled minister of that place, having married Miss Susannah Smith, the daughter of the Rev. John Smith, of White Plains, Westchester county, and State of New York, on the 16th of May, 1750. I remember my grandparents very well, having visited them often when I was young. Of their pedigree I know but little, but have heard my grandfather Tallmadge say that his father, with a brother, left England together, and came to this country, one settling at East Hampton, on Long Island, and the other at Branford, in Connecticut. My father descended from the latter stock. My father was born at New Haven, in this State, January 1st, 1725, and graduated at Yale College, in the year 1747, and was ordained at Brookhaven, or Setauket, in the year 1753, where he remained during his life. He died at the same place on the 5th of February, 1786. My mother died April 21st, 1768, leaving the following children, viz. :

WILLIAM TALLMADGE, born October 17, 1752, died in the British prison, 1776.

BENJAMIN TALLMADGE, born February 25, 1754, who writes this memoranda.

SAMUEL TALLMADGE, born November 23, 1755, died April 1, 1825.

JOHN TALLMADGE, born September 19, 1757, died February 24, 1823.

ISAAC TALLMADGE, born February 25, 1762.

My honored father married, for his second wife, Miss Zipporah Strong, January 3rd, 1770, by whom he had no children.

Having, from childhood, exhibited an eager desire for learning, my father determined to give me the opportunity to obtain a liberal education, and as he was preparing a number of boys for college, he placed me as a student among them, and when I was twelve years old, I had acquired such a knowledge in classical learning, that President Dagget, on a visit to my father, examined and admitted me as qualified to enter college, when I was twelve or thirteen years old. My father deemed it improper for me to go to college so young, and, therefore, kept me at home until the Autumn of 1769, when I became a member of Yale College.

Being so well versed in the Latin and Greek languages, I had not much occasion to study during the two first years of my collegiate life, which I have always thought had a tendency to make me idle, when, if I had rightly improved my time, it would have afforded me an opportunity for improvement in other sciences.

It, however, served to induce me to *Dean's* bounty, which I should have been a candidate for, had not the measles wholly prevented me from studying during a part of my junior and senior years.

At the commencement of 1773, I took my first degree, having had an honorable appointment by the President, the Rev. Dr. Dagget, to speak publicly on the occasion.

Having had an application to superintend the *High School* in Weathersfield, then about to become vacant by the retirement of David Humphreys, Esq., I accepted the same, and repaired to that place for the purpose. I was very much gratified and pleased, both with my employment and the people, and continued there until the commencement of the revolutionary war. When first American blood was shed at Lexington by the British troops, and again repeated much more copiously at Bunker's Hill, near Boston, the whole country seemed to be electrified. Among others, I caught the flame which was thus spreading from breast to breast, and mounted my horse to go and see what was going on near Boston. I soon found my friend, Capt. Chester, of Weathersfield, who had been at Bunker's Hill, in the late conflict. He first intimated to me the idea of joining the army. Although I was sufficiently ardent to be pleased, and even elated with such a prospect, yet nothing was further from my intention at that time than to have entered upon a military life.

While I was at Cambridge with my military friends, I was continually importuned to think of the oppression which was so abundantly exhibited by the British government towards the Colonies, until I finally became entirely devoted to the cause in which my country was compelled to engage. I finally began to think seriously of putting on the uniform, and returned to Weathersfield full of zeal in the cause of my country. After my return to Connecticut, the prospect of peace and reconciliation appeared to be almost hopeless, and the country began to think seriously of raising an army to oppose the British troops wherever they should be located. Congress apportioned to the then Colonies their several quotas of troops, and the State of Connecticut, by their legislature, resolved to raise their proportion of men, in the year 1776, for the campaign of 1776.

Capt. Chester, before mentioned, was appointed a colonel, and he immediately offered me the commission of a lieutenant, with the appointment of adjutant to his regiment. My feelings had been so much excited, that I was gratified by this offer from my friend, and decided at once to lay aside my books (having almost determined to study law), and take up the sword in defense of my country. My lieutenant's commission, signed by the venerable Gov. John Trumbull, was dated June 20th, 1776, and my warrant as adjutant bore the same date.

Having now commenced my new profession of arms, and believing myself influenced by the most patriotic principles, I waited the orders of my commander, ready to go wherever he should order. The British fleet, under the command of Admiral Shuldham, and the army commanded by General Howe, had left Boston, or gone to Halifax, and were at sea. General Washington expected the enemy would make their next appearance at New York, and had put the American army under march for that city. I obtained permission to visit my father at Brookhaven, on my way to New York, and I shall not soon forget his surprise at seeing me dressed in military uniform, with epaulets on my shoulders, and a sword by my side. Although he was a firm and decided whig of the revolution, yet he seemed very reluctant to have me enter the army. However, the die was cast, and I soon left the paternal abode and entered the tented field.

While the British fleet and army were at sea, or at Halifax, my duties were almost constant and unceasing, in training and disciplining our newly raised regiment for the service of the field the ensuing campaign. My ambition was almost boundless, and my health and spirits being of the first order, I felt ready to do or undergo almost any service that might be assigned to me.

We arrived at the city of New York in the month of June, 1776, and my place of regimental parade was assigned in Wall Street, where, every morning and evening, the regiment assembled for exercise. During the heat of the day, the men were excused from duty, the heat being too intense to be borne by them in the sun. The American army. composed principally of levies, or troops raised for short periods, and militia, had now assembled at New York, and in its vicinity, when it was announced that a large British fleet was discovered off the Hook, on the 29th of June. In a few days, the British fleet entered the Hook, and Sir William Howe, who commanded the army, landed on Staten Island, where, by the arrival of Lord Howe, he had a force about twenty-five thousand men. The newly furnished troops, consisting of foreigners and native subjects, having now joined those who had recently left Boston, General Washington (having arrived also from Boston) began to introduce system and order into the heterogeneous mass of troops that had been brought into the field, and were placed under his command. The war now put on a very serious aspect, as independence had been declared, and it seemed no longer doubtful that the contest on which we had entered must be decided by the sword.

The British commissioners (of which Lord Howe was one), however, opened their commission by addressing a letter to General Washington in his *private character*, and forwarded the same to our Commander-in-Chief by Colonel Patterson. General Washington refused to receive these dispatches for the want of respectful address, and returned them to the commissioners, unopened, assigning the foregoing reasons for his refusal. The army was highly gratified by this conduct of General Washington, and Congress publicly approved of the same on the 17th of July, 1776.

The Declaration of Independence, which had been solemnly adopted by Congress on the Fourth of July, 1776, was announced to the army in general orders, and filled every one with enthusiastic zeal, as the point was now forever settled, and there was no further hope of reconciliation and dependence on the mother country.

The movements of the enemy indicating an intention to approach New York by the way of Long Island, Gen. Washington ordered about 10,000 men to embark and cross the East River at Brooklyn. The regiment to which I belonged was among the first that crossed over, and, on the 27th of August, the whole British army, consisting of their own native troops, Hessians, Brunswickers, Waldeckers, etc., to the number of at least 25,000 men, with a most formidable train of field artillery, landed near Flatbush, under cover of their shipping, and moved towards Jamaica and Brooklyn. As our troops had advanced to meet the enemy, the action soon commenced, and was continued, at intervals, through most of the day. Before such an overwhelming force of disciplined troops, our small band could not maintain their ground, and the main body retired within their lines at Brooklyn, while a body of Long Island Militia, under Gen. Woodhull, took their stand at Jamaica. Here Gen. Woodhull was taken prisoner and inhumanly killed. The main body of our army, under Major-Gen. Sullivan and Lord Stirling, fought in detached bodies, and on the retreat both of those officers were made prisoners. I also lost a brother the same day, who fell into their hands, and was afterwards literally starved to death in one of their prisons; nor would the enemy suffer relief from his friends to be afforded to him.

This was the first time in my life that I had witnessed the awful scene of a battle, when man was engaged to destroy his fellow-man. I well remember my sensations on the occasion, for they were solemn beyond description, and very hardly could I bring my mind to be willing to attempt the life of a fellow-creature. Our army having retired behind their intrenchment, which extended from Vanbrunt's Mills, on the West, to the East River, flanked occasionally by redoubts, the British army took their position, in full array, directly in front of our position. Our intrenchment was so weak, that it is most wonderful the British General did not attempt to storm it soon after the battle, in which his troops had been victorious. Gen. Washington was so fully aware of the perilous situation of this division of his army, that he immediately convened a council of war, at which the propriety of retiring to New York was decided on. After sustaining incessant fatigue and constant watchfulness for two days and nights, attended by heavy rain, exposed every moment to an attack from a vastly superior force in front, and to be cut off from the possibility of retreat to New York by the fleet, which might enter the East River, on the night of the 29th of August, Gen. Washington commenced recrossing his troops from Brooklyn to New York. To move so large a body of troops, with all their necessary appendages, across a river full a mile wide, with a rapid current, in face of a victorious, well disciplined army, nearly three times as numerous as his own, and a fleet capable of stopping the navigation, so that not one boat could have passed over, seemed to present most formidable obstacles. But, in face of these difficulties, the Commander-in-Chief so arranged his business, that on the evening of the 29th, by 10 o'clock, the troops began to retire from the lines in such a manner that no chasm was made in the lines, but as one regiment left their station on guard, the remaining troops moved to the right and left and filled up the vacancies, while Gen. Washington took his station at the ferry, and superintended the embarkation of the troops. It was one of the most anxious, busy nights that I ever recollect, and being the third in which hardly any of us had closed our eyes to sleep, we were all greatly fatigued. As the dawn of the next day approached, those of us who remained in the trenches became very anxious for our own safety, and when the dawn appeared there were several regiments still on duty. At this time a very dense fog began to rise, and it seemed to settle in a peculiar manner over both encampments. I recollect this peculiar providential occurrence perfectly well; and so very dense was the atmosphere that I could scarcely discern a man at six yards' distance.

When the sun rose we had just received orders to leave the lines, but before we reached the ferry, the Commander-in-Chief sent one of his Aids to order the regiment to repair again to their former station on the lines. Col. Chester immediately faced to the right about and returned, where we tarried until the sun had risen, but the fog remained as dense as ever. Finally, the second order arrived for the regiment to retire, and we very joyfully bid those trenches a long adieu. When we reached Brooklyn ferry, the boats had not returned from their last trip, but they very soon appeared and took the whole regiment over to New York; and I think I saw Gen. Washington on the ferry stairs when I stepped into one of the last boats that received the troops. I left my horse tied to a post at the ferry.

The troops having now all safely reached New York, and the fog continuing as thick as ever, I began to think of my favorite horse, and requested leave to return and bring him off. Having obtained permission, I called for a crew of volunteers to go with me, and guiding the boat myself, I obtained my horse and got off some distance into the river before the enemy appeared in Brooklyn.

As soon as they reached the ferry we were saluted merrily from their musketry, and finally by their field pieces; but we returned in safety. In the history of warfare I do not recollect a more fortunate retreat. After all, the providential appearance of the fog saved a part of our army from being captured, and certainly myself, among others who formed the rear guard. Gen. Washington has never received the credit which was due to him for this wise and most fortunate measure.

When the enemy had taken possession of the heights opposite the city, they commenced firing from their artillery, and the fleet were in motion to take possession of those waters, which, had it been done a little earlier, this division of our army must inevitably have fallen into their hands.

In a day or two after, the British army began to move up the Island to Hurl Gate, when it became manifest that their object was to cut off the retreat of our troops from New York. My first station was at Turtle Bay, on York Island. A British frigate having taken her station in the East River, we began to fire upon her from a small battery of eighteen pounders, and did her some damage. As soon as she got springs on her cable, however, she began so heavy a fire upon our redoubt, that in less than thirty minutes she entirely dismounted our guns, and we were glad to leave so uncomfortable a place.

My next halt was at our battery at Hurl Gate, opposite to which, on Long Island, the enemy erected a battery of heavy cannon, from which they commenced a tremendous fire on our fort, and soon made a breach in it, and dismounted most of our guns. After this, they began to make preparations for crossing the East River. Gen. Washington immediately put his army in motion to leave the city, the stores, etc., etc., having been previously removed. Both rivers, viz., the North and the East, were now filled with British shipping, and boats were seen passing from Long Island to New York, filled with soldiers, who formed and deployed immediately after landing. A considerable body of our troops had not yet retired from the city; but being hastened by this movement of the enemy, took the North River road, and thus escaped being entirely cut off. Some skirmishing ensued, which proved of little consequence. In the course of the day, a portion of our brigade, under Gen. Wadsworth, was engaged, and our Brigade-Major, *Major Wyllis*, was made a prisoner. I was immediately appointed to fill his station, and entered on my new duties.

Gen. Washington halted on the heights between Harlem and Kingsbridge, and the enemy appeared in full force on the South, or opposite side of Harlem. While in these situations, detachments from the two armies had frequent skirmishes, which produced no very important results.

It was not long before the British troops were found to be

recrossing the East River to Long Island, and moving to the East. This induced Gen. Washington to remove his army off from York Island, and take a new position in the county of Westchester, North and East from Kingsbridge, leaving garrisons in forts Washington and Lee, located on both sides of the North, or Hudson River. In this new position we remained for some time, no important event having taken place. As the enemy showed a disposition to cross over into Westchester, Gen. Washington removed the main body of his army up to the White Plains, taking possession of the high ground North and East of the town. Here he seemed determined to take his stand, his lines extending from a mountain on the right, called Chadderton's Hill, to a lake or large pond of water on his left. An intrenchment was thrown up from right to left, behind which our army formed. Long poles with iron pikes upon them, supplied the want of bayonets. Chadderton's Hill was separated from the right of our intrenchment by a valley of some extent, with the river Bronx directly before it; but being within cannon shot of our intrenchment on the right, Gen. Washington thought it best to occupy it, and ordered Gen. McDougall, with 800 or 1,000 men, to defend it, and if driven from it, to retire upon the right of the line. The American army were all at their several posts on the last September and beginning of October; and here it looked as if Gen. Washington intended to give battle to the British army. On the 27th October, 1776, it was announced at Head Quarters that the enemy was in motion from Westchester, through Eastchester, directly toward the White Plains. A detachment of 2,000 or 3,000 men was ordered to proceed on the old York road to meet the enemy in front. As *our brigade* formed a part of the force, I, of course, was among them. Before the dawn of day, on the 28th of October, we learned that the enemy were in full march directly in front of us. Gen. Spencer, who commanded this body of troops in advance, immediately made the necessary disposition to receive the enemy, having the river Bronx on our right, and between us and the troops on Chadderton's Hill. At the dawn of day, the Hessian column advanced within musket shot of our troops, when a full discharge of muskety warned them of their danger. At first they fell back, but rallyed again immediately, and the column of British troops having advanced upon our left, made it necessary to retire. As stone walls were frequent, our troops occasionally formed behind them, and poured a destructive fire into the Hessian ranks. It, however, became necessary to retreat wholly before such an overwhelming force. To gain Chadderton's Hill, it became necessary to cross the Bronx, which was fordable at that place. The troops immediately entered the river and ascended the hill, while I being in the rear, and mounted on horseback, endeavored to hasten the last of our troops, the Hessians being then within musket shot. When I reached the bank of the river, and was about to enter it, our Chaplain, the Rev. Dr. Trumbull, sprang up behind me on my horse, and came with such force to carry me with my accoutrements, together with himself, headlong into the river. This so entirely disconcerted me, that by the time I reached the opposite bank of the river, the Hessian troops were about to enter it, and considered me as their prisoner. As we ascended the hill, I filed off to the right, expecting our troops on the hill would soon give them a volley. When they had advanced within a few yards of a stone wall, behind which Gen. McDougall had placed them, our troops poured upon the Hessian column, under Gen. Rahl, such a destructive fire, that they retreated down the hill in disorder, leaving a considerable number of the corps on the field. This relieved me from my perilous situation, and I immediately remounted my horse, and taking my course in the valley, directly between the hostile armies, I rode to Head Quarters, near the Court-house, and informed Gen. Washington of the situation of the troops on Chadderton's Hill. The enemy having rallied, and being reinforced, made a second attempt upon Gen. McDougall's detachment, who gave them a second warm reception; but, being overpowered, retired upon the right of our line, then in order of battle. A severe cannonade was kept up from both armies through the day, and every moment did we expect the enemy would have attempted to force us from our lines. In the meantime, Gen. Washington had begun to remove his stores and heavy baggage up to Northcastle.

After remaining in our lines and on constant military duty for several days and nights, on the 1st of November Gen. Washington retired with his army to the heights in the neighborhood of Northcastle. Thus baffled, Gen. Howe gave over the pursuit, and began his march towards Kingsbridge, where he assembled his troops to invest Fort Washington. In the mean time, Gen. Washington apprehending that the enemy would immediately attempt the capture of forts Washington and Lee (two strong fortifications on each bank of the Hudson and below Kingsbridge), ordered his troops into the vicinity of Peekskill, on the North River. After stationing suitable guards on the Croton river, and to protect the country from plunder, etc., Gen. Washington crossed the Hudson with a considerable portion of his troops, and removed down into the neighborhood of Fort Lee. After a most desperate assault on Fort Washington by the Hessian troops under Gen. Kniphausen, aided by different corps of the British under the command of Gen. Mathews, Col. Stirling, and Lord Percy, and the outposts of the garrison being driven in, and their ammunition almost expended, Col. Morgan, who commanded in the garrison, beat a parley and surrendered. By this unfortunate event, we lost about 3,000 men, a great part of whom perished in prison by severe usage, sickness, etc.

After the fall of Fort Washington, it became certain that Fort Lee could not be sustained, and as Lord Cornwallis had crossed the Hudson River at Dobb's ferry, and above the fort, it became necessary to be on the alert. The troops at and in the neighborhood of Fort Lee, moved off in season to avoid the approach of the enemy, and retired over the Hackensack River, into the State of New Jersey. This was a period of great dismay. The campaign of 1776 was now drawing to a close, and the periods for which the American troops had been enlisted, were daily expiring. The enemy had been victorious, and flushed with success, were insolent and cruel both to the inhabitants and to their prisoners. In fact, all was confusion and dismay, and it seemed as if we were on the eve of despair and ruin.

If I was writing a history of the revolutionary war, I

should not fail in this momentous period of our revolution to notice the events which transpired in the Northern army and on the Lakes.

The attacks on Charleston, South Carolina, at the South, and the lodgment of a British force at Newport, R. I., in all which places, except before Charleston, disasters and dismay seemed to be the portion of America. But, as I was noticing only some of the prominent events of my own life, and those which took place where I have been providentially placed (*quorum pars fui*), I will not enlarge.

The New England troops being left on the East side of the Hudson, or North River, and Gen. Washington, with the Southern troops principally, having taken his course to the South, halted occasionally as he passed through New Jersey, but kept before the enemy until they crossed the river Delaware. This river then became the boundary or dividing line between the two armies. The enemy soon took possession of Trenton, Bordentown, and Burlington, which places were occupied principally by the Hessian troops. The British troops occupied Princeton, New Brunswick, and Amboy. To the troops on the East side of the North River was appropriated the service of calling the attention of the enemy to their front at Kingsbridge, Harlem, etc., to call off their pursuit of Gen. Washington, and his broken corps. But the period of discharge of this division of the army was at hand, as the year was now at its close, and Congress had finally determined to raise an army for the war, on the pressing recommendation of Gen. Washington. In the Fall of the year 1776, Congress resolved to raise eighty-eight battalions of infantry, and apportioned to each State in the Union its quota of these troops. In the month of December they resolved to raise four regiments of horse, and sixteen additional regiments of infantry, authorizing Gen. Washington to appoint officers for the whole of them. This produced an entire change in all our military system, and those who felt ardent in their country's cause, were now called upon to step forward and engage in her service. Before our regiment was dismissed, I had the offer of the first troop, in the 2d regiment of light dragoons, commanded by Colonel Elisha

Sheldon. As these appointments were from Gen. Washington, I felt highly honored and gratified by the appointment, and before the levies were dismissed, I enlisted the quota of men for my troop. My commission as captain bore date the 14th of December, 1776, and was signed by John Hancock, President. I had now entered upon a new career, both as to the nature and the duration of my military service. The dragoon service being so honorable and so desirable, it became an object of primary importance to obtain an appointment in this corps. I now left my fellow-officers of the infantry, and proceeded to Philadelphia to receive instructions from the Board of War about raising and equipping this new body of troops. As I passed on, Gen. Washington had planned his expedition against the Hessians at Trenton, in which he captured about one thousand men, on the night of the 25th of December, and the next day recrossed the Delaware with his troops and prisoners. This event gave a new force to our affairs, and where gloom and dismay prevailed, zeal and courage began to appear. This fortunate attack upon the enemy at Trenton, inspired the militia with such courage, and they flocked to the American camp in such numbers, that Gen. Washington determined again to cross the Delaware at Trenton, of which he took possession. The British troops having now collected at New Brunswick and Princeton, Lord Cornwallis, with a select body of troops, was dispatched to attack the American army. He entered Trenton on the 2d of January, 1777 ; and on that day Gen. Washington retired across the river at Trenton, called the Assumpink, which divides the town, running from East to West, and then falls into the Delaware. After making several fruitless attempts to pass the river at the bridge and fording-places, to attack our troops, Cornwallis halted on the North side of the river, intending to make the attack the next day. Aware of his danger, Gen. Washington caused the fires of his encampment to be kept up, and suitable sentinels and patrols to be on duty through the night, while, with the main body of his troops, he filed off to the right, and the next morning at day-break was at Princeton. There he found three regiments of British troops, which he immediately engaged and dispersed, killing and taking about four hundred men, of which more than one hundred were slain. Our loss in killed was about the same, among whom was Gen. Mercer, of Virginia. As soon as Lord Cornwallis found that Gen. Washington had eluded him, he moved his troops from Trenton to Princeton, on their way to New Brunswick. The rear of our troops had scarcely left Princeton, when the vanguard of the British entered, between which some shots were exchanged. Gen. Washington crossed the Millstone, destroying all the bridges, which greatly retarded the enemy. Turning to the North, toward Somerset Court House, he left Lord Cornwallis to pursue his march to New Brunswick, where his stores and baggage were deposited, and our little army halted for refreshment and repose. In a short time Gen. Washington removed the remains of his army to Morristown, N. J., where he took up his Winter quarters. Thus the campaign of 1776 closed with honor to the American arms, although a considerable portion of it had been replete with disaster.

It being determined that the 2nd Regiment of Light Dragoons, to which I was attached, should rendezvous at Wethersfield, in Connecticut, I proceeded to that place, where all recruits were ordered to assemble. There I immediately erected a large circular *Manage*, for the purpose of training and breaking our horses, and the Winter and ensuing Spring were occupied in preparing for the campaign of 1777, which, from all preparations making on both sides, bid fair to be a bloody one. As soon as the Spring had opened, and traveling became practicable, Gen. Howe began to show a disposition to take the field. Gen. Washington removed his army forward from Morristown to the strong and elevated positions North of Middlebrook. There he intrenched and fortified his encampment, and awaited the movements of the enemy.

Gen. Washington, foreseeing the intention of Gen. Howe to strike some decisive blow with such a powerful military force as he had at command, had directed that all recruits should be forwarded to Head Quarters as fast as they were collected. He also sent a particular order to Col. Sheldon to send on all the effective men of his regiment. Having about men and horses enough to form four troops, they were accordingly put in the best order, and the command of the *squadron* was given to me, as senior Captain in the regiment. My own troop was composed entirely of *dapple gray horses*, which, with black straps and black bear-skin holster-covers, looked superb. I have no hesitation in ackowledging that I was very proud of this command.

At the opening of the campaign of 1777, I moved off with this noble body of horse from Weathersfield, where I had passed a very pleasant and a very active and busy Winter. My military duties by day, and the pleasant intercourse with the inhabitants in the evening, made the time pass rapidly away. I left the place and the people with some regret, but being fired with military ambition and panting for glory, I took up my line of march—passing through Farmington, Harrington, Litchfield, and Kent, in Connecticut, and from thence to Peekskill and King's Ferry, where we crossed the Hudson River. Thence by Haverstraw, the Clove, and Pompton to Morristown, where Gen. Washington had encamped his army through the preceding Winter. From this place I reported my detachment to the Commander-in-Chief, who ordered me to move on the next day to his encampment near Middlebrook, where he reviewed us and commended the appearance of my detachment.

The day following, all the light horse, consisting of Col. Blond's, Col. Maylan's, and my squadron, were ordered to parade, and proceeded down to Woodbridge to reconnoitre the enemy. After we came in full view of them, they immediately got under arms. Pretty soon some of their light troops appeared to be filing off to the right and left, and quickly appeared in our rear. Our next attempt was to pass through their *corps*, which we did, each squadron taking a separate course. Our loss was but small, considering the fire we sustained. After this we retired towards Head Quarters, and halted for the night, being covered by Col, Morgan's Regiment of Riflemen. Early next morning, being June 25, 1777, our patrols came in, announcing the approach of the enemy. As soon as the dragoons could be mounted, the enemy was in sight, and the firing commenced, which began the battle of the Short Hills.

Lord Stirling commanded the left wing of the advanced division of our army, and fell in with Lord Cornwallis, who commanded the grenadiers and light infantry of the British army. In the course of the battle four field pieces were taken from Lord Stirling, and again retaken and finally lost. The main body of the enemy, under Gen. Howe, did not fall in with Gen. Washington, who immediately took possession of his strongholds back of Middlebrook. Thus the British General was disappointed in his plan of drawing Gen. Washington into a general battle. Our light troops hovered upon the rear of the enemy until they reached Elizabethtown. After this Gen. Howe drew in his out-posts, and pretty soon began to embark his army for their southern expedition. As soon as Gen. Washington could determine the course that the British fleet had steered, he put his whole army under march for the Delaware. The fleet left the Hook on the 23rd of July, 1777. The destination of my squadron was to Carrol's Ferry over the Delaware, which I reached in good season. By this time the remainder of our recruits had come on, and we had a fine body of dragoons in the field. The army crossed the Delaware, and the whole body moved on slowly towards Philadelphia, and halted at Germantown. There Gen. Washington anxiously waited to know the destination of the British fleet and army.

By this time I was promoted to the rank of Major in the 2nd Regiment Light Dragoons, my commission being dated from the time of the vacancy, viz., April 7, 1777. I now gave up the command of my favorite troop, taking my station as field officer in the regiment. Gen. Washington having ascertained that the British fleet had steered to the South after they left Sandy Hook, was finally informed they had actually entered, and were proceeding up the Chesapeake Bay. On the 25th of August, Gen. Howe landed his army, about twenty thousand strong, on the East side of the Chesapeake Bay, near the head of the Elk, so called, near French Town. On the 27th the troops were put in motion towards Philadelphia.

When Gen. Washington put his army in motion, we were about eighteen thousand strong. After passing through the principal streets of Philadelphia, we continued our march until we reached

Wilmington. As the enemy advanced, Gen. Washington took his station on the left bank, or on the North side of the Brandywine, near which river it appeared probable that the hostile armies must engage, as they had now advanced within a few miles of each other. On the morning of the 11th of September, 1777, Gen. Howe put his army in order of battle, and moved on towards the Brandywine. By 10 o'clock in the morning the action commenced, and was sustained from right to left by turns through the whole line. The action was obstinate on both sides, and lasted through the day ; but the left wing of the British army having crossed the river, some distance above, on the right of our army, came down upon our right, while the Hessians crossed in front at Chadsford, and the American troops were forced to retire. The action lasted through the day, and at night Gen. Washington took his station at Chester, and the British army remained in possession of the field. The next day Gen. Washington retired to Philadelphia, and the British army extended their right wing into Wilmington. Finding Philadelphia not to be capable of defense against such a powerful foe, Gen. Washington retreated to the high grounds about Germantown, while Gen. Howe advanced to the right bank of the Schuylkill, opposite to Philadelphia. Some of our light troops hung upon his left wing and rear, to prevent their predatory excursions. The bridges over the Schuylkill having been removed, Gen. Howe moved up the right, or western bank of that river. Gen. Washington having recrossed the Schuylkill, determined, on the 16th of September, again to meet Gen. Howe in the field of battle. The arrangements were made, and the advance parties had already commenced firing, when there came on a violent shower of rain, which unfitted both armies for action. Gen. Washington now recrossed the Schuylkill, and encamped on the eastern side of that river. Gen. Howe, learning that Gen. Wayne was on his left, within a few miles of him, with about 1500 men, near the *Paola Tavern*, on the Lancaster road, detached Gen. Gray, with a select corps of light troops, to surprise him. This he accomplished so effectually, that he forced his way into the midst of Wayne's detachment before he was discovered. A dreadful slaughter ensued, in which the sick and wounded were killed indiscriminately with those who were taken in arms. Gen. Howe moved still higher up the Schuylkill, as if he would go to Reading, where we had much military stores collected. Gen. Washington removed his army to Pottsgrove ; this gave the enemy an opportunity to ford the Schuylkill at the fords above the bridges, and their march to Philadelphia was open and easy, on the 23rd of September ; and on the 26th, Lord Cornwallis entered that city at the head of a column of British and Hessian grenadiers. Congress, a few days before, adjourned from Philadelphia to meet at Lancaster, from whence they removed over the Susquehanna River and sat at Yorktown. The main body of the British army now encamped at Germantown, and Gen. Washington posted his army about 16 miles North of Germantown, on the Shippack Creek. Efforts were now made to draw in all detachments of the army, and to collect a force that might enable Gen. Washington to cope with the adversary. Although defeated at the Brandywine, and foiled in several smaller rencounters, our American Fabius retained his full determination to give these hostile invaders no repose. Having learned that Cornwallis was stationed at Philadelphia with about 5,000 troops, while the main body was posted in a line from East to West at Germantown, with their light troops in front and on the flanks, Gen. Washington determined to attack them. The arrangement and order of battle was such, that if every division of the army had performed its allotted part, it seems as if we must have succeeded. Such was the order of battle, that the front, the flanks, and even the rear of the British encampment, were to have been attacked at the same time. My own position was at the head of Gen. Sullivan's division, on the left of the centre ; Gen. Wayne being on our right, and the Commander-in-Chief in the centre of both divisions, which was the centre of the army. Having marched from our camp on the evening of the 3rd of October, '77, by 3 o'clock the next morning we found ourselves close in upon the scene of action. Just before the dawn of day, the troops were put in motion, and in a few moments the firing commenced. The out-posts and advanced guards of the enemy were driven in with great precipitation, and by 9 o'clock we found ourselves almost in the heart of Germantown. A very heavy fog prevented our *corps* from discovering one another, so as to distinguish, in some cases, friend from foe. Hitherto the progress of our troops had been entirely successful, and it seemed as if the victory must be ours. Some of the regiments on the flanks had reached the centre of the village, and had then more prisoners than troops of their own ; and in this situation, finding themselves separated from their own brigades, were captured by the enemy.

At this critical moment, Col. Musgrave, of the British army, threw his regiment into a large stone house directly in front of our division in the centre, from which he poured a heavy and galling fire upon our troops. All attempts to dislodge them were ineffectual, and although they would have been harmless in a few minutes if we had passed them by, yet through the importunity of Gen. Knox (which I distinctly heard), Gen. Washington permitted him to bring his field artillery to bear upon it, but without effect. During this transaction time elapsed, the situation of our troops was uncomfortable, their ardor abated, and the enemy obtained time to rally. In less than thirty minutes, our troops began to retire, and from the ardor of pursuit, were in full retreat. This not being general through the line, of necessity left the flanks of some divisions and brigades uncovered and exposed to the assaults of an exasperated foe. From this moment the prospects of victory were changed, and notwithstanding all our attempts to rally the retiring troops, it seemed impossible to effect it, even by the presence of the Commander-in-Chief. I threw my squadron of horse across the road, by order of Gen. Washington, repeatedly, to prevent the retreat of the infantry ; but it was ineffectual. In addition to this, after our attack had commenced, Lord Cornwallis had commenced his march from Philadelphia with the grenadiers and light troops, and had reached Germantown. This relieved the enemy greatly ; but they pursued us very cautiously. After our army had passed Chestnut Hill, the enemy halted, as did also our troops. Thus, in an unexpected moment, when everything seemed to look favorable to our cause, victory was turned into defeat, and the fugitive enemy was the cautiously pursuing foe. Gen. Washington fell back to his old quarters at Shippack, where the dispersed troops assembled, and the enemy retired to Philadelphia. In the meantime, Lord Howe had assembled his fleet in the Delaware Bay, and as the obstructions which had been placed in the river below Philadelphia, to prevent the progress of the fleet, still remained, and the army were obliged to depend on the fleet for all their provisions, it became necessary that these obstructions should be removed. The *chevaux de frise* could not be removed so long as our forts protected them. It therefore became necessary that Mud Island Fort, forts Mifflin and Mercer in the river, and the fort at Red Bank, on the Jersey shore, should be taken by the enemy, while the English troops attacked the forts on the islands in the river. A corps of Hessians, under Col. Donop, crossed the Delaware at Cooper's Ferry, opposite to Philadelphia, to attack the fortress at Red Bank. These different divisions of troops were put in motion on the evening of the 21st of October, '77. The next day the several attacks commenced. The cannonade was so heavy from the forts and the ships, that we heard it distinctly at our encampment, about 40 miles distant. Col. Donop approached Red Bank with great gallantry, with a strong and select corps of Hessian troops, who entered the entrenchments of the outer works, but failed in attempting to scale the inner fort, into which our troops had retired. From this they found so heavy and so destructive a fire, that the enemy were obliged to retire, leaving their Colonel and Commander mortally wounded, and a prisoner, and 400 or 500 men on the field of battle. The second officer in command was also wounded. Lieut. Col. Linsing drew off the remainder with precipitation, and returned to Philadelphia totally defeated. The other attempts also failed of success. But the wants of the army became so pressing that further attempts became necessary to remove these obstructions. A portion of the navy, as well as of the army, was assigned to this service, which met with varied success, some of the ships being totally destroyed. After awhile, the men-of-war drawing near, and forts being erected to rake our batteries, it was found necessary to abandon them, which was accordingly done with little loss of men. From this time the intercourse with the fleet by the Delaware River was unobstructed and free.

Our Northern army, under Gen. Gates, having been victorious, and Gen. Burgoyne and his whole army, having been made prisoners, the continental troops that had served in that army were ordered to join the army under Gen. Washington. This they effected in the latter part of November, soon after which Gen. Washington determined to look at Gen. Howe again in the field. About the 1st of December he removed his whole army from Shippack down to White Marsh, occupying the strong grounds on the North side of the flat ground known by that name. On the morning of the 4th of December, Gen. Howe came out with the whole British army, and encamped at Chestnut Hill, directly in front of our right wing. Having now so respectable a force in the field (about 15,000 strong), and especially the Northern army being flushed with recent victory, and hoping that the other troops would vie with them in the contest, a battle was rather desired than avoided. After continuing several days in his first position, by day-break on the 7th, Gen. Howe took a new position in front of our left wing, on the flank of which I was posted with a body of horse, together with Morgan's Light Infantry and Riflemen. We came into contact with the British light infantry and dragoons, in which Major Morris, of our infantry, was killed. I thought a general battle was inevitable, but neither General thought it prudent to descend into the plain. After continuing in this position a few days, Gen. Howe retired to Philadelphia for Winter quarters, to our great wonder. Shortly after, Gen. Washington repaired to Valley Forge, on the West side of the Schuylkill, and encamped for the Winter. The soldiers were obliged to make log huts to shelter them from the inclemencies of the weather, and very few of them had a blanket to cover them. Indeed, the whole army were in great want of the most necessary articles of clothing, and many of them had no shoes to their feet, so that they could be tracked by the blood which they left on the ground as they constructed their huts. Thus closed the campaign of 1777, the most sanguinary of any that took place during the war.

As soon as our army had encamped, late in the month of December, 1777, the Commander-in-Chief stationed me with a respectable detachment of dragoons, as an advanced corps of observation between our army and that of the enemy. I had to scour the country from the Schuylkill to the Delaware River, about five or six miles, for the double purpose of watching the movements of the enemy and preventing the disaffected from carrying supplies of provisions to Philadelphia. My duties were very arduous, not being able to tarry long in a place, by reason of the British light horse, which continually patrolled this intermediate ground. Indeed it was unsafe to permit the dragoons to unsaddle their horses for an hour, and very rarely did I tarry in the same place through the night.

While on this duty, at about 2 o'clock in the morning, I was attacked by a large body of British light horse, commanded by Lord Rawdon. So long as the battle lasted in the road, we made good our defense ; but when they leaped the fences, and got upon our flanks, we were obliged to retreat. Our loss was small, not exceeding 3 or 4 killed, and as many wounded. Soon after this, being informed that a *country girl* had gone into Philadelphia, with eggs, instructed to obtain some information respecting the enemy, I moved my detachment to Germantown, where they halted, while, with a small detachment, I advanced several miles towards the British lines, and dismounted at a tavern called the *Rising Sun,* in full view of their out-posts. Very soon I saw a young female coming out from the city, who also came to the same tavern. After we had made ourselves known to each other, and while she was communicating some intelligence to me, I was informed that the British light horse were advancing. Stepping to the door, I saw them at full speed chasing in my patrols, one of whom they took. I immediately mounted, when I found the young damsel close by my side, entreating that I would protect her. Having not a moment to reflect, I desired her to mount behind me, and in this way I brought her off more than three miles up to Germantown, where she dismounted. During the whole ride, although there was considerable firing of pistols, and not a little wheeling and charging, she remained unmoved, and never once complained of fear after she mounted my horse. I was delighted with this transaction, and received many compliments from those who became acquainted with it.

After my command in the lines before Philadelphia closed, which was in January, 1778, the light horse having been ordered to Trenton, I repaired to that place with my detachment, and from thence the 2nd Regiment Light Dragoons removed to Chatham, New Jersey, for Winter quarters. Here we were permitted to rest from the fatigues of a severe and bloody campaign. But our brethren at Valley Forge passed a Winter of extreme suffering, being in want of provisions and clothing to an alarming degree. Gen. Washington, however, was constantly engaged in providing for his suffering troops, and in recruiting his army for the ensuing campaign.

In the meantime, Gen. Clinton succeeded Gen. Howe at Philadelphia (1778). Early in the Spring, the enemy making some movements on the Hudson, our regiment was ordered to leave their Winter quarters at Chatham, and proceed towards the Clove and King's Ferry, to watch their motions.

In the latter part of May, or beginning of June, 1778, we took up our line of march to open another campaign, feeling somewhat like veteran troops, after such a campaign as the last. In June, it became evident to Gen. Washington that the British army was about to remove from Philadelphia. On the 22d of June, 1778, Gen. Henry Clinton, by the aid of the shipping, removed his army from Philadelphia, and landed at Gloucester Point, in New Jersey. Gen. Washington immediately broke up his camp at Valley Forge, and after despatching several light corps to hang upon the flanks and rear of the enemy, he moved with his main body and crossed the Delaware River at Cargell's Ferry, when it became manifest that Gen. Clinton would take the road to New York through Monmouth.

Gen. Washington put his whole force in motion, to fall in if possible with the enemy at that place. Gen. Lee, who had been recently exchanged, having the command of the light troops, was directed to attack the enemy, and harrass them until the Commander-in-Chief could come up with the main body of the army. Being pressed on all sides by our light troops, Gen. Clinton was obliged to face about upon Gen. Lee's division, which soon began to retire. At this critical moment Gen. Washington came up, and was astonished to find Lee's corps on the retreat. After delivering some pretty stern remarks to Lee, he immediately endeavored to restore the order of the battle, and soon checked the progress of the enemy's troops. The conflict became very heavy and dubious for a time, until the enemy, in turn, gave way, and Gen. Washington gained the ground that Lee had abandoned. The conflict continued through the day from Monmouth to Freehold, when night parted the combatants. Our army slept on the field of battle, and Gen. Washington intended to have renewed the contest the next morning ; but Gen. Clinton, aware of his danger, took advantage of the darkness and cool of the night, and moved off towards Middletown, whither his baggage, under the escort of Gen. Kniphausen, had been sent forward. By this night's march, Gen. Clinton had escaped the vigilance of Gen. Washington, and on the 30th of June he arrived at Sandy Hook, where Lord Howe had arrived with his fleet, ready to receive and convey the troops to New York. In the battle of Monmouth, or Freehold, the British lost about 1,000 men, 400 or 500 of whom were killed. The American loss did not exceed 200 or 300 men. Many died on both sides from excessive heat and fatigue—the day being oppressively warm, and the troops drinking too freely of cold water.

The battle was greatly in favor of the Americans, although had Washington's orders been obeyed, the victory would doubtless have been much more decisive. Gen. Lee was soon afterwards arrested by Gen. Washington on three charges, found guilty, and suspended from command for twelve months. Gen. Washington, as well as Congress, commended the conduct of the army, and returned thanks, etc.

On the 1st of July, Gen. Washington took up his march for the Hudson, to guard the passes of the Highlands, and soon the main army again assembled together on the East side of the Hudson.

France having entered into an alliance with the United States after the capture of Burgoyne's army, had sent out a formidable fleet under the Count De Estaing, which entered the mouth of the Delaware Bay on the 8th of July. If he had reached that station a few days sooner, the fleet from Philadelphia must have fallen into his hands, and most probably the British army would have been captured. The Count soon learned the destination of the British fleet, and on the 11th of July he appeared off Sandy Hook, in face of Lord Howe and the British fleet, who did not venture out for action. After tarrying before the Hook a few days, the French fleet stood out to sea, and soon appeared before the harbor of Newport, R. I.

The British troops under Gen. Pigot, now began to be in jeopardy. An army of 10,000 men was promptly assembled, and took possession of the high ground North of Newport, and by the coöperation of the French fleet, the British garrison, about 6,000 strong, must inevitably have been taken. But Lord Howe appearing off the inlet, the French Admiral put to sea in quest of him—a storm coming on, both fleets were dispersed and much injured, which prevented a naval battle ; and the French fleet retired again to Newport. In a few days, however, the French Admiral informed Gen. Sullivan that he was going to Boston to refit. Notwithstanding all the entreaties and expostulations of Gens. Sullivan, Greene, and Lafayette, the French fleet weighed anchor, and on the 2d of August set sail for Boston. Thus exposed to the British fleet, and such reinforcements as Gen. Clinton might send for from New York, Gen. Sullivan was obliged to retire from the island and take a position on the main land.

This year (1778) I opened a private correspondence with some persons in New York (for Gen. Washington) which lasted through the war. How beneficial it was to the Commander-in-Chief is evidenced by his continuing the same to the close of the war. I kept one or more boats continually employed in crossing the Sound on this business.

My station during the campaign of 1778, was in the county of Westchester, and occasionally along the shores of the Sound. No important blow was given the enemy during this campaign, by the American army, although the light troops in advance (as was always the case with our regiment) were frequently in conflict with similar corps of the enemy.

When the campaign closed, our regiment went to Durham, in Connecticut, for Winter quarters. A part of the time, however, I was from choice stationed at Greenfield, from whence I could easily cross to Long Island.

During the Summer of 1779, Gov. Tryon was despatched with 2,000 or 3,000 troops, and a protecting naval force, to distress the seaports of Connecticut. He landed at New Haven, and pillaged the town, After some skirmishing he embarked his troops, and next visited and burnt the handsome town of Fairfield. Taking the next town in course, he also burnt and utterly destroyed Norwalk. Finding him bent on such a desolating expedition, I was despatched with a body of light infantry to aid the militia in defending the latter place. The enemy approached the town at break of day, and immediately set it on fire. The scene was awful—to see the inhabitants—men, women, and children—leaving their houses, and fleeing before the enemy, while our troops were endeavoring to protect them.

They embarked again the same day at sunset, and returned to New York, after having experienced pretty uncivil treatment while they were at Norwalk.

From Norwalk I moved my detachment, and encamped them on both sides of the Hudson. Gen. Clinton. in the month of of May, having viewed the importance of navigating the Hudson in its true light, embarked the flower of his army and proceeded up the North River. After investing the American posts on Verplank's Point, and Stony Point, the former surrendered, and the garrison in the latter made their escape. These fortifications are nearly opposite to each other, on the banks of the Hudson, at King's Ferry, near Haverstraw— Stony Point being on the West side of the river, and Verplank's Point on the East. Gen. Washington having assembled his army in the neighborhood of these plains, conceived the idea of driving the enemy from them. The enemy had made the fort at Stony Point impregnable, as they supposed, and had placed in it a garrison of select troops, about 600 strong. A body of our light infantry, about 1,000 strong, under the command of Gen. Wayne, moved forward on the 15th of July, 1779, and soon after midnight were ordered to commence the attack in two columns. As soon as we were discovered by the garrison, they commenced a tremendous fire of musketry and cannon, while not a gun was discharged by any of our troops. Such was the ardor and impetuosity of the Americans, that they surmounted all difficulties, removed all obstructions, cut away the abatis and a double stockade, mounted the ramparts, and captured the whole garrison in a short time with the bayonet alone. Although the fire was so heavy from the fortress, our loss of men was comparatively small, while that of the enemy, in slain, was very considerable.

Gen. Robert Howe, with his troops (of which our regiment made a part), on the East side of the Hudson, moved up in view of the fort on Verplank's Point, as if to attack it, and then retired, which he did repeatedly, to my utter astonishment, supposing that we were to attack it. It was afterwards said that this operation was a feint, to divert the attention of the garrison from Stony Point.

After the object of this movement was accomplished, my detachment, and indeed the whole of our regiment, took their station in the region of the White Plains, Northcastle, etc., as a sort of advance guard to the army.

Our parties and those of the enemy had frequent interviews, and sometimes not of the most friendly nature. I had been nearly led into an ambuscade by the enemy in an excursion down upon the lines. My orders were to go into Westchester, but by some means the enemy got information of my intended expedition, and threw a large body of infantry into a thicket on the road. I got knowledge of the movement just before the troops reached the spot, and retired without loss.

On my way back to the regiment, my brave Sergeant-Major, James Dole, was shot by one of the Cow-boys. The bullet entered on one side, just above the hip, and came out on the other—passing directly through his body. As soon as I saw him, I supposed he was mortally wounded; but he finally recovered, and served to the close of the revolutionary war, and lived many years after.

At the commencement of this campaign, our regiment was ordered to its old station on the lines, below Bedford, North-castle, etc. Not long after we took the field, about July 1, 1779, Lord Rawdon, with nearly all the British light horse, accompanied by a body of light infantry, made an attack upon our corps in the night. The onset was violent, and the conflict carried on principally with the broad sword, until the light infantry appeared upon our flanks, when Col. Sheldon found it necessary to retreat. This was done with so much celerity, that the enemy gained but little advantage. I lost in the affray a fine horse, most of my field baggage, and twenty guineas in cash, which were taken in my valise with my horse.

Before the campaign closed, viz., on the 5th of September, 1779, I undertook an expedition against the enemy on Lloyd's Neck, on Long Island. At this place, and on a promontory or elevated piece of ground next to the Sound, between Hunting-ton Harbor and Oyster Bay, the enemy had established a strong fortified post, where they kept a body of about 500 troops. In the rear of this garrison a large band of maraud-ers encamped, who, having boats at command, continually in-fested the Sound and our shores. Having a great desire to break up this band of freebooters, on the evening of said 5th of September I embarked my detachment, amounting in the whole to about 130 men, at Shipam Point, near Stamford, at 8 o'clock in the evening, and by 10 we landed on Lloyd's Neck. Having made my arrangements, we proceeded in differ-ent divisions to beat up their quarters. Our attack was so sudden and unexpected, that we succeeded in capturing almost the whole party—a few only escaping into the bushes, from whence they commenced firing on my detachment, which gave the alarm to the garrison. This prevented our attempting any attack upon the out-posts and guards of the fort, and after destroying all the boats we could find, as well as the huts of those refugees, we returned with our prisoners to our boats, and embarked for Connecticut, where we landed in safety before sunrise the next morning, and without the loss of a single man. (See the copy of my letter to Gen. Robert Howe, dated September 6th, 1779.)

At the close of the campaign, our regiment went to North Hampton for Winter quarters, and I was appointed to meet the Commissioners of the State of Connecticut at Weathersfield, to adjust and settle the *depreciation* of the pay of their troops.

In the course of the last campaign (1779) we were made joyful by the arrival of the French army, about 6,000 strong, under the command of the Count Rochambeau. As they arrived at Newport, in Rhode Island, they immediately debarked and fortified themselves in that place.

Having now decisive evidence that our august ally, Louis XVI., had determined to afford us efficient aid, we considered the independence of our country *absolutety sure.* A large fleet was also expected with a further reinforcement of troops.

This gave us strong hopes that the next campaign would prove to be a vigorous and a decisive one. The pay to the army being entirely in *continental paper*, we were greatly embarrassed to procure even the necessary supplies of food and clothing.

The main body of our army encamped on both sides of the Hudson, from Tappan, in New Jersey, to Verplank's Point and the Croton. In this campaign the enemy extended their posts, East on Long Island, for the double purpose of maintaining an *illicit intercourse* with the people of Connecticut, and also that they might protect their foraging parties down Long Island.

Having constant and repeated intelligence from New York, and all parts of Long Island, I began to entertain the plan of breaking up the whole system. I commenced by stating to the Commander-in-Chief the situation of the different fortifications, the marauding parties going down the island, and the unceasing intercourse of our community with New York, etc., etc.

3

After this, I began to intimate my plans for beating up the enemy's quarters, and disturbing their repose. To all this Gen. Washington listened with kind attention, and I felt almost prepared to make a direct application to cross the Sound with a detachment of troops.

In the course of the Summer of 1780, Gen. Washington honored me with a separate command, consisting of the dismounted dragoons of our regiment and a body of horse. Our dismounted dragoons had been formed into two companies of light infantry, and were commanded by excellent officers, who, to a man, rejoiced in the idea of separate and active duty. I removed my fine detachment of light troops over towards Horse Neck, from whence I took a station at New Canaan, or North Stamford. This gave me an opportunity to watch the enemy, either up on the lines, or across the Sound on Long Island. While my detachment laid in this situation, Gen. Parsons proposed to me to aid him in the capture of the enemy's fort and garrison on Lloyd's Neck, opposite to Stamford, on Long Island. He had with him a very select detachment from the Connecticut line, of about 700 men. I readily acceeded to his proposal, and held my detachment ready for the enterprise.

In the meantime, the General sent over a refugee to gain the needed intelligence, and directed him to meet him at a given place, and at a time appointed.

Just before the time had arrived to commence our operations, the General proposed to me to take the command of the expedition. As he communicated to me his plan of obtaining the needed intelligence, I was alarmed at the character of his agent, especially as he was within the enemy's lines. On the whole, I thought it best to decline the honor of the command, but offered to take my detachment under his orders. This put an end to the expedition, and afterwards we learned, that on the night we had appointed to cross, a large body of the garrison were stationed at the place appointed for our landing, which probably would have annoyed us greatly.

After this, I took my station again upon the line, in the county of Westchester. After marching, and counter-marching, skirmishing with the enemy, catching cow-boys, etc., etc., late in the month of September, viz., on the evening of the 23rd, I returned from below to the regiment, then near Northcastle. Soon after I halted, and disposed of my detachment, I was informed that a prisoner had been brought in that day by the name of John Anderson. On inquiry, I found that three men by the names of John Paulding, David Williams, and Isaac Van Vert, who had passed below our ordinary military patrols, on the road from Tarrytown to Kingsbridge, had fallen in with this John Anderson, on his way to New York. They took him aside for examination, and discovering sundry papers upon him, which he had concealed in his boots, they determined to detain him as a prisoner, notwithstanding Anderson's offers of pecuniary satisfaction if they would permit him to proceed on his course. They determined to bring him up to the head-quarters of our regiment, then on the advanced post of our army, and near Northcastle. This they effected on the forenoon of the 23rd day of September, 1780, by delivering said Anderson to Lieut.-Col. John Jameson, of the 2nd Regiment Light Dragoons, then the commanding officer of said post, Col. Sheldon being at old Salem, under arrest.

His Excellency Gen. Washington had made an appointment to meet the Count Rochambeau (who commanded the French army then at Newport, R. I.,) at Hartford, in Connecticut, about the 18th or 20th of September, and was on his return to the army at the time of Anderson's capture. When I reached Lieut.-Col. Jameson's quarters, late in the evening of the 23rd, and learned the circumstances of the capture of the prisoner, I was very much surprised to find that he had been sent by Lieut.-Col. Jameson to Arnold's head-quarters at West Point, accompanied by a letter of information respecting his capture. At the same time he dispatched an express with the papers found on John Anderson, to meet Gen. Washington, then on his way to West Point. I did not fail to state the glaring inconsistency of this conduct to Lieut.-Col. Jameson, in a private and most friendly manner. He appeared greatly agitated when I suggested to him a measure which I wished to adopt, offering to take the whole responsibility upon myself, and which he deemed too perilous to permit. I will not further disclose. I finally obtained his reluctant consent to have the prisoner brought back to our head-quarters. When the order was about to be dispatched to the officer to bring the prisoner back, strange as it may seem, Lieut.-Col. Jameson *would persist* in his purpose of letting his letter go on to Gen. Arnold. The letter did go on, and the prisoner returned before the next morning.

As soon as I saw Anderson, and especially after I saw him walk (as he did almost constantly) across the floor, I became impressed with the belief that he had been *bred to arms*. I communicated my suspicion to Lieut. Col. Jameson, and requested him to notice his gait, especially when he turned on his heel to retrace his course across the room.

It was deemed best to remove the prisoner to Salem, and I was to escort him. I was constantly in the room with him, and he soon became very conversable and extremely interesting. It was very manifest that his agitation and anxiety were great. After dinner on the 24th, perhaps by three o'clock P. M., he asked to be favored with a *pen, and ink, and paper*, which I readily granted, and he wrote the letter to Gen. Washington, dated "Salem, 24th September, 1780," which is recorded in most of the histories of this eventful period. In this letter he disclosed his true character to be " *Major John Andre, Adjutant-General to the British Army.* "

When I received and read the letter (for he handed it to me as soon as he had written it), my agitation was extreme, and my emotions wholly indescribable. If the letter of information had not gone to Gen. Arnold, I should not have hesitated for a moment in my purpose, but I knew it must reach him before I could possibly get to West Point.

The express sent with the papers found in Major Andre's boots, did not intercept Gen. Washington on his return from Hartford, but passed him on the road, and kept on to West Point. On the 25th, while at breakfast with two of Gen. Washington's *Aids*, who had actually arrived at his quarters, Arnold received the letter from Lieut.-Col. Jameson. Knowing that the Commander-in-Chief would soon be there, he immediately rode down to his boat, and was rowed down the

North River to the British sloop-of-war, *Vulture*, which then lay in Tappan Bay, below King's Ferry. This was the same vessel that brought up Major Andre from New York. Not long after Arnold's abrupt and sudden departure from his quarters, at Robinson's House, on the East side of the Hudson, opposite to West Point, the express delivered the despatches to Gen. Washington, who immediately repaired to Arnold's quarters. By this time the plot was all discovered, and the guilty traitor had escaped. I took on Major Andre, under a strong escort of cavalry, to West Point, and the next day I proceeded down the Hudson to King's Ferry, and landed at Haverstraw, on the West side of the Hudson, where a large escort of cavalry had been sent from the main army at Tappan, with which I escorted the prisoner to Head-Quarters.

After we arrived at Head-Quarters, I reported myself to Gen. Washington, who ordered a court consisting of fourteen general officers, to sit and hear the case of Major Andre. On the 29th of September, the president of the court (Gen. Greene) reported to the Commander-in-Chief that they had come to the conclusion, "that Major Andre, Adjutant-General to the British Army, ought to be considered as a spy from the enemy, and that, agreeably to the law and usage of nations, it is their opinion that he ought to suffer death."

On the 30th of September, the Commander-in-Chief, in general orders, approved of the aforesaid opinion, and ordered that the execution should take place, *the next day, at 5 o'clock P. M.*

On the first of October, 1780, a vast concourse of people assembled to witness the solemn and affecting scene, when the execution was postponed, in consequence of a flag having arrived from the enemy. Gen. Greene was appointed to meet Gen. Robertson at Dobb's Ferry ; but as no satisfactory proposals were received from Gen. Robertson, Gen. Greene returned to Head-Quarters and reported to Gen. Washington. The Commander-in-Chief then ordered that the execution should take place on the 2nd of October. Major Andre, having received his regimentals from New York, appeared in the complete uniform of a British officer, and, in truth, he was a most elegant and accomplished gentleman. After he was informed of his sentence, he showed no signs of perturbed emotions, but wrote a most touching and finished letter to Gen. Washington, requesting that the mode of his death might be adapted to the feelings of a man of honor. The universal usage of nations having affixed to the crime of a *spy*, *death by the gibbet*, his request could not be granted. As I was with him most of the time from his capture, and walked with him as he went to the place of execution, I never discovered any emotions of fear respecting his future destiny before I reached Tappan, nor of emotion when his sentence was made known to him. When he came within sight of the gibbet, he appeared to be *startled*, and inquired with some emotion whether he was not to be shot. Being informed that the mode first appointed for his death could not consistently be altered, he exclaimed, " How hard is my fate!" but immediately added, " it will soon be over." I then shook hands with him under the gallows and retired.

Major Andre was executed in his military uniform, in which, I think, he was laid in his coffin, but before he was interred, I feel satisfied that his servant took off his coat, and perhaps other outer garments.

If it comported with the plan of these memoranda, and I could trust my feelings, I might enlarge greatly in anecdotes relating to this momentous event in our revolutionary war, and especially those which relate to this most accomplished young man. Some things relating to the detention of Andre, after he had been sent on to Gen. Arnold, are purposely omitted, and some confidential communications which took place, of a more private nature, serve rather to mark the ingenuous character of the man, than to require being noticed at this time. I will, however, remark, that for the few days of intimate intercourse I had with him, which was from the time of his being brought brought back to our head-quarters to the day of his execution, I became so deeply attached to Major Andre, that I can remember no instance where my affections were so fully absorbed in any man. When I saw him swinging under the gibbet, it seemed for a time as if I could not support it. All the spectators seemed to be overwhelmed by the affecting spectacle, and many were suffused in tears. There did not appear to be one hardened or indifferent spectator in all the multitude.

The next day after the execution of Major Andre, October 3rd, 1780, I set out on my return to rejoin my detachment in the county of Westchester. There my duties became very arduous, the late events having excited much rage on the part of the enemy. What with *cow-boys*, *skinners*, and *refugees*, we had as much as we could turn our hands to, to keep from being waylaid and fired upon from thickets and stony eminences, about Salem, Northcastle, and White Plains. Indeed, it was not an unusual thing to have our sentinels fired on from parties who would crawl up in the darkness of the night, and then disappear.

As soon as I had settled again in the course of our duties, my former scheme of annoying the enemy on Long Island came fresh upon my mind. I therefore directed my agents there to obtain for me the most accurate returns of the fortifications in Suffolk county, Long Island, at a point which projects into South Bay, on Smith's Manor, being their most easterly point of defense. This I found to be a triangular inclosure of several acres of ground, at two angles of which was a strong barricade house, and at the third, a fort, with a deep ditch and wall encircled by an abatis of sharpened pickets, projecting at an angle of 45 degrees. The fort and houses were entirely connected by a strong stockade, quite high, and every post sharpened, and fastened to each other by a transverse rail strongly bolted to each. The works were nearly finished, when I proposed to the Commander-in-Chief to let me go over and demolish the same. He heard me with pleasure, but on the whole concluded that the danger attending the whole expedition was too great to warrant the undertaking. My hopes being disappointed for that time, I did not abandon the project, but continued my inquiries on Long Island. Towards the last of October, or the beginning of November, 1780, I determined to cross the Sound myself, and go over to Long Island for the purpose of obtaining intelligence. This I accomplished and returned in safety. Among other things, I learned that the fortress at Smith's Manor was completed—that it was the depository of stores, dry goods, groceries, and arms, from whence Suffolk county could be supplied ; and the works presented, on the whole, a most formidable appearance.

Having now procured an accurate draft of Fort St. George, as delineated on a small scale on the foregoing page, and also .information that a large quantity of hay and forage had been collected by the enemy at Corum, from the East end of Long Island, I began urgently to importune Gen. Washington to permit me to capture the fort and destroy the magazine of forage.

On the 11th of November he answered my letter, and authorized the enterprise. All necessary preparations being made, on the 21st of November, 1780, at about 4 o'clock P. M., I embarked my detachment, composed of two companies of dismounted dragoons, and in all short of 100 selected men, at Fairfield, and the same evening, at 9 o'clock, we landed at a place on Long Island, called the *Old Man's*. I was obliged to go thus far East, to avoid a large body of the enemy which lay at Huntington and its vicinity, in our direct course from Stamford. Soon after we landed, say by 10 o'clock, I put the troops in motion to cross Long Island. We had not gone far, say four or five miles, before the wind began to blow from the southeast, and the rain soon followed. I faced the troops about, returned to our boats, which were drawn up and placed in the bushes for concealment. There we remained through the night, and the next day, at evening, the rain abated, and I ordered the troops to march for our destined place on the South side of Long Island. At 4 o'clock next morning, I found we were within two miles of Fort St. George. We halted for a short time to take a little refreshment. Having made my arrangements for the plan of attack, I placed two small detachments under the command of subaltern officers of high spirit, at different positions from the fort, with orders to keep concealed until the enemy should fire on my column. Just as the day began to dawn I put my detachment in motion. The pioneers, who preceded my column, had reached within 40 yards of the stockade before they were discovered by the enemy. At this moment, the sentinel in advance of the stockade, halted his march, looked attentively at our column, and demanded " Who comes there ?" and fired. Before the smoke from his gun had cleared his vision, my sergeant, who marched by my side, reached him with his bayonet, and prostrated him. This was the signal for the other detachments to move forward, when all seemed to vie with each other to enter the fort. So resolute were the troops, that a break was soon made in the stockade, where the rear platoon halted to prevent the prisoners from escaping. I led the column directly through the Grand Parade against the main fort, which we carried with the bayonet, in less than ten minutes, not a musket being loaded. At the same instant that I entered on one side of the fort, the officers commanding the two smaller detachments mounted the ramparts on the other side, and the watch-word, " *Washington and glory*," was repeated from three points of the fort at the same time. While we were standing, elated with victory, in the centre of the fort, a volley of musketry was discharged from the windows of one of the large houses, which induced me to order my whole detachment to load and return the fire. I soon found it necessary to lead the column directly to the house, which, being strongly barricaded, required the aid of the pioneers with their axes. As soon as the troops could enter, the confusion and conflict were great. A considerable portion of those who had fired after the fort was taken, and the colors had been struck, were thrown headlong from the windows of the second story to the ground. Having forfeited their lives by the usages of war, all would have been killed had I not ordered the slaughter to cease. The prisoners being secured, it was soon discovered that the shipping which lay near to that fort, loaded with stores, etc., were getting under way. The guns in the fort were brought to bear on them, and they were soon secured. All things were now secured and quiet, and I had never seen the sun rise more pleasantly. It now became necessary to demolish the enemy's works, as far as possible, which was done. An immense quantity of stores, of various kinds, was destroyed. The shipping and their stores were also burnt up. Some valuable articles of dry goods were made up in bundles, placed on the prisoners' shoulders, who were pinioned two and two together, and thus carried across the island to our boats. The work of capturing and destroying this fortress being effected, at 8 o'clock A. M. I put the troops under march to re-cross the island to our boats. Having given the command of the detachment to Capt. Edgar, with orders to halt at a given point at the middle of the island, I selected ten or twelve men, and mounted them on horses taken at the fort, with which I intended to destroy the King's magazine at Corum. This place was nearly half way to the place where a large detachment of British troops was encamped, East from Huntington. I reached the place in about an hour and a half, made a vigorous charge upon the guard placed to protect the magazine, set it all on fire, and in about one and a half hours more reached the place where I had ordered the detachment to halt, having ridden about 16 miles.

When I arrived at the rendezvous, I was gratified to see the head of the detachment under Capt. Edgar, with the prisoners, just then advancing. As none of us had halted since we parted, we sat down for nearly an hour and refreshed. After this we took up our line of march again, and by 4 o'clock reached our boats. These we soon put into the water, and before the sun set we were all afloat on the Sound, heading for the port whence we embarked.

By midnight, or about 1 o'clock the next morning, every boat arrived at Fairfield beach, although we had entirely lost sight of each other by reason of the darkness of the night.

This service was executed without the loss of a man from my detachment, and one only was badly wounded, and him we brought off. The enemy's loss was seven killed and wounded, the most of them mortally. We took one lieut.-colonel, the commandant, one lieutenant, one surgeon, and fifty rank and file, with a host of others in the garrison. (See Journals of Congress, December 4th and 6th, 1780, vol. vi.)

No person but a military man knows how to appreciate the honor bestowed, when the Commander-in-Chief and the Congress of the United States return thanks for a military achievement. On this occasion, the most honorable mention was made by both, and conveyed in the most flattering manner.

After the troops were recruited, say in two or three days, I moved my detachment to their former station on the line. On this duty we continued until late in December, when the regiment repaired to Simsbury and Windsor for Winter quarters.

Operations on the lines having ceased, and both armies, as if by common consent, having gone into quarters, my business as well as inclination led me to move into the vicinity of the Sound, that I might find some spot where the common enemy might be annoyed.

I pretty soon conceived the idea, and suggested to Gen. Washington the plan, of taking Lloyd's Neck Fort and its neighboring fortress, about 8 miles eastward on Long Island. When the campaign was about commencing, I opened my mind fully to the Commander-in-Chief, in a letter dated April 6th, 1781, and he having expressed a favorable opinion of the enterprise, about the 22nd of April I concluded once more to go over to Long Island, to obtain the best information I could get respecting the enemy's posts, their strength in troops, and works, in the hope that I might soon be permitted to go over and beat up their quarters. This I accomplished, and informed Gen. Washington that by the aid of a small naval force, say two frigates, the Sound could be cleared, and with his permission I would take my own detachment, and such additional force as he should judge necessary, and break up their establishment at Lloyd's Neck, of about 800 men, and Fort Slongo, of about 150 men.

Gen. Washington immediately furnished me with a very flattering introduction to Count Rochambeau, then at Rhode Island, and permitted me to be the bearer of it. I immediately set off for Newport, about 140 miles distant, where I arrived April 22nd, and was most favorably received by Count Rochambeau, who commanded the French army, and the Chevalier Destouches, who commanded the French fleet. The absence of the smaller ships of the squadron, on special service, prevented the execution of the plan.

The enterprise was of necessity abandoned for the time, and I again returned to my command on the lines. As the French army was expected to take the field with us in this campaign, great exertions were made to put the troops in the best order.

I proceeded to Hartford, to procure horses and accoutrements for our regiment, and while there the van of the French army arrived, on their way to our camp. On the 25th of June, 1781, the French army left Hartford, passing through Farmington, Woodbury, Newton, etc., to Bedford. I soon followed, and when they were near the lines, the light troops of our army, met the French army, and Gen. Washington moved down with a fine body of troops, to look at the enemy at Kingsbridge. The *red-coats* got under arms, and seemed to act as if they expected an attack.

We continued in view of each other throughout the day, and then retired for repose. The next day, the same maneuver took place, and I presume there were many in both *corps* who wished the British troops to leave their strong entrenchments beyond Kingsbridge, and give the allied force an opportunity to pay their respects to them. As Sir Henry Clinton very prudently kept within his own fortified encampment, Gen. Washington directed the troops to retire towards White Plains on the left, and Tarrytown on the right. In this situation the army remained for some time, viz., through the month of July, and past the middle of August. About the 20th of August, the army was again ordered to be in readiness to march. The common opinion was, that our movement was to be toward Kingsbridge, where some pretty serious work was expected. It soon appeared that the main body of the combined forces was moving up the Hudson, and when the troops reached King's Ferry they began to cross the river.

Sheldon's Regiment of Dragoons was continued on the lines in the county of Westchester, and a part of the infantry, under Gen. Heath, was stationed in the Highlands, about Peekskill and West Point. Gen. Washington having his own plan of operations, entirely deceived the British General, by marching his combined force down New Jersey opposite to New York, as if he intended an investment of that city. After maneuvering a few days in September opposite to Staten Island. of a sudden the whole army were found in full march for the Delaware

River, which they crossed at Trenton, and then proceeded on to the head of the Elk, where they embarked to move down the Chesapeake Bay for Yorktown, where Lord Cornwallis had taken his station.

While the army was on its march and at Philadelphia, the pleasing intelligence was received that Count De Grasse, with 36 sail of the line, had arrived in the Chesapeake Bay, with 3,000 land troops on board. Every exertion was now made to hasten on the troops, and before the close of September the combined army had reached their place of destination, and Gen. Washington commenced in form the seige of Yorktown.

This seige was carried on with great vigor, parallel after parallel being laid out, and the intrenchments completed, while the two advanced redoubts of the enemy had been taken by storm.

On the 18th of October, 1781, Lord Cornwallis sent out a flag proposing a capitulation, asking for 24 hours to settle the preliminaries. Gen. Washington replied and allowed 12 hours. On the 19th his Lordship surrendered his whole army of 7,247 effective men. The total number who capitulated (including wounded, and the sick in hospital) may probably be fairly rated at 11,000 men—75 pieces of brass, and 169 pieces of iron ordnance, with 7,794 muskets were also surrendered.

Never was mortification greater than this haughty, cruel, plundering army exhibited on this humiliating occasion. The joy and exultation were proportionally great in the allied army, although not the smallest insult was offered to the prisoners. The terms of the capitulation, and other incidents connected with it, are recorded in history, which I purposely omit.

As light dragoons were not needed in a seige, for the first time since the Continental army was raised, our regiment was not under the immediate command of Gen. Washington. I returned to my own command.

As the army on the East side of the North River was greatly weakened by the march of the main body to Virginia, our duty on the lines was of course very severe. Having been honored by the Commander-in-Chief with a separate command, I moved wherever duty seemed to call. My former plan of annoying the enemy on the Sound, and on Long Island, came fresh to my recollection.

The fortress at Treadwell's Neck, called Fort Slango, seemed to demand attention, as the next in course to Fort St. George which we had already taken. On the 1st of October, I moved my detachment of light infantry into the neighborhood of Norwalk. At the same time I directed a suitable number of boats to assemble at the mouth of the Saugatuck River, East of the town of Norwalk, and on the evening of the 2nd of October, 1781, at 9 o'clock, I embarked a part of my detachment, and placed Major Trescot at the head of it, with orders to assail the fort at a particular point.

The troops landed on Long Island by 4 o'clock, and at the dawn of day the attack was made and the fortress subdued. The blockhouse and other combustible materials were burnt, and the detachment and prisoners returned in safety.

Soon after this I returned to my old station on the lines about the White Plains, where we found enough to do to protect the inhabitants against the refugee corps, under Col. Delancy, at Westchester, and the cow-boys, and skinners who infested the lines. On similar service the remainder of the campaign was employed, while the combined army under the victorious Washington, returned from the capture of Lord Cornwallis and once more took up their quarters on both sides of the Hudson.

The campaign having again opened (1782), the general opinion was that the toils and perils of the war would soon close, and that peace might soon be looked for to terminate the struggle. The country seemed already to feel as if our independence was sure, and as if little effort was now needed to consummate the work.

Whatever might have been the private opinion of Gen. Washington, he impressed upon the army the necessity of strict discipline, that the troops might be prepared for any emergency. A reform of the army having taken place, and many supernumerary officers having been permitted to retire, the phalanx that remained in the field was organized anew, and we felt able to contend with the enemy on any ground. In fact it became an object of solicitude to come in contact with the foe at any time.

The enemy now keeping very much within their lines, they gave us but few opportunities to reach them in combat. As the war appeared to be drawing to a close, the spirit of trade and intercourse with New York seemed greatly to increase. My detachment was therefore posted near the Sound, from whence we occasionally visited Horseneck, and the plains on the lines in the county of Westchester, where driving cattle to the enemy, etc., was a business of almost constant employment. Gen. Carlton having succeeded to the command of the British army, and pursuing a peaceful policy, greatly increased the intercourse. But my orders being very strict to prevent it, we were kept on pretty close duty through this campaign. Towards the close of the campaign, a detachment of British troops, about 600 strong, came down Long Island into Suffolk county and encamped at Huntington, as if for Winter quarters.

As soon as I was informed of this fact, I endeavored to obtain the fullest particulars ; and having learned that a considerable portion of the British light horse, covered by a body of infantry, had taken up their quarters at Huntington, on the North side of Long Island, I conceived the plan of beating up their quarters. It was about the 20th of November, 1782, when they felt safe from any attack from our side of the water, and more from the lateness of the season. Having matured my plan, I disclosed it to the Commander-in-Chief, and requested his permission to go over and accomplish my object. I even went to Head-Quarters, and had a personal interview with Gen. Washington on this subject. Having obtained his permission to undertake the expedition about the first of December, I began to make the necessary arrangements to carry this my favorite plan into execution. I was, however, informed by Gen. Washington, that although I might collect my boats, so as to give no alarm, I must not undertake to execute the plan, before he named to me the precise time. My order finally came, naming the night of the 5th of December, 1782. The fact was, Gen. Washington had planned an expedition down the North River at the same time. His intention was to have thrown a large detachment of his army below Fort Washington, while he moved down with the main body to Fort Independence and Kingsbridge. The enemy thus placed between two fires, would have been forced to yield, while, with my detachment on Long Island, they would have found themselves attacked on all sides.

My detachment consisted of four companies of light infantry—chosen troops—and a body of dismounted dragoons, to mount the captured horses of the enemy. I had also a body of Connecticut levies attached to my command, amounting in all to about 700 men. On the evening of the 5th of December, 1782, the different detachments met (for the first time) in the vicinity of Stamford, from whence they moved on to Shipan Point, where I had ordered the boats to assemble. Here, finding such preparations, the officers first began to suspect that something pretty serious was going on. When the sun had set, the weather being severe, I ordered the whole detachment to parade on the shore, where our little fleet had assembled. As soon as the platoons were assigned to each boat, they began to embark, but before one-half of the troops had entered the boats, I discovered a squall of wind rising from the West, accompanied by rain, which, from its violence, made it necessary to halt and disembark the troops which had entered the boats. The violence of the wind and rain, mixed with snow, continued through the night, so that we were obliged to draw up our boats and turn them over to protect the troops from the pelting storm. The next morning the rain had ceased, but the face of the Sound was a perfect foam, so that no boat could have been kept above water for five minutes. The wind lasted through the day, and at sunset it somewhat abated, so that I ordered the troops again to parade. A few of the boats were put into the water, but the wind rising again, we were obliged to desist. The second night was spent in the same manner as the first, and the next day I was informed that three boats from Long Island had taken refuge on one of the Norwalk islands, a few miles to the eastward of us, wind-bound like ourselves, and could not return. The wind and sea abating somewhat of their violence, and the enemy's boats appearing on the Sound returning to Long Island, I ordered six of my best boats (with sails) to be manned, and Capt.

Brewster, an experienced sailor, was directed to look up the enemy, and if possible to capture them. The boats put off from the shore, and although their course was before the wind, three of them were obliged to turn back. The enemy seeing our boats bearing down upon them, pressed all sail as well as oars, and steered for Long Island.

Capt. Brewster steered his course so judiciously, that before they had reached the middle of the Sound (being here about 12 miles wide) he fell in with two of their heaviest boats, when they engaged with great fury. On the first fire, every man in one of the enemy's boats fell, being either killed or wounded. Capt. Brewster received a ball in his breast, which passed through his body. He, however, captured the two boats, and one escaped. Although we supposed Capt. Brewster mortally wounded, yet he recovered, and lived to be nearly 80 years old.

On the third night I determined, if possible, to cross the Sound, and with the same flattering prospects when the sun set, I made preparations to embark the troops, when the wind rising again most furiously, I was constrained to give over the expedition, which became the more advisable as one of the enemy's boats had escaped, and probably had given the information that a body of our troops were on Shipan Point.

The next day I removed my detachment and put them under march for camp. On the 8th of December, 1782, I made my .report to Gen. Washington, more severely mortified and chagrined than I had ever been in my life. A letter in reply from Gen. Washington, dated December 10, 1782, fully approving my conduct, served to raise my spirits again.

What added greatly to my mortification, was the knowledge that my enterprise was a part of another, much more important, on the North River and below Fort Washington, stated a little back ; but I soon learned that this enterprise also failed. On the day previous to the evening when the troops were to have passed down the river, some British ships anchored above Fort Washington, so that no boats could pass by them undiscovered. I cannot say but even this great disappointment gave me some relief under my own providential prevention. But what is

4

most worthy of notice, is the fact that when these two attempts were to have been made, in which doubtless many lives would have been lost, the preliminary articles of peace had been actually signed.   This was not known to us.

The campaign having now closed, I took my old station upon the shores of the Sound.   Through my private emissaries, I obtained much information respecting the illicit trade carried ˑ on to Long Island, etc., and many of these trading boats fell into our hands.   One adventure I must relate, from the singular circumstances which accompanied it.   In the course of the Winter, I was informed that one of our public armed vessels, which was appointed to cruise in the Sound to protect our commerce and to prevent the illicit trade (technically called the *London trade*), was actually engaged in carrying it on.   She was a large sloop called the *Shuldham*, armed and equipped, and commanded, I think, by Capt. Hoyt.   I hardly knew how to suspect him, but having been minutely informed of the invoice of her goods, and that she would be at Norwalk on a given day, I felt in duty bound, under my orders, to watch her.   I repaired to Norwalk with a few dragoons, and finding said sloop coming up the harbor, I took out a warrant, got a constable, and when she anchored below at the *Old Wells*, I got a boat and went on board.   After due salutations were passed, I took the captain into the cabin and informed him of my suspicions and errand.   He flew into a great passion, and first threatened to throw me overboard.   I endeavored to satisfy him . of the futility of such threats, and ordered him, by virtue of my superior military rank, to obey my commands.   He immediately ordered the anchor to be weighed and the sails hoisted, and stood out to sea, with a smart wind at northwest.   I ordered him to put back, but he refused, and swore most vehemently that he would throw me overboard, when I assured him if he made any such attempt I would certainly take him along with me.   My captain continued his course towards Lloyd's Neck, where the enemy's fleet lay, until we had reached about the middle of the Sound.   I inquired of him where he was going, when he informed me, with an oath, that he would carry me over to the enemy.   I informed him that for such an offense, by our martial law, he exposed himself to *the punishment of death.*

He professed to care nothing for the consequences, and swore he would do it. I maintained my former course, and very sternly ordered him to put about his vessel and return to Norwalk, assuring him that if he executed his threat I would have him hanged as high as Haman hung, if I ever returned, as I did not doubt I should. The time now became critical, for we were rapidly approaching the enemy, when I again demanded that he should put about his ship and return. He now began to hesitate, and in a few minutes he ordered his men to their posts, and put his vessel about and steered directly back into Norwalk harbor. As soon as he came to anchor down at *Old Wells*, so called, the captain went ashore in his boat, and I never saw him again. I now found myself in the peaceable possession of the vessel and its cargo. On taking up the scuttle in the cabin, I found the assortment of English goods agreeably to my invoice, which I had duly libeled and con. demned. Thus ended my hazardous contest with the captain of the *Shuldham*, who must have been a man void of principle, and wholly unworthy the commission he held.

On the 20th January, 1783, we captured several boats with goods, etc., both foreign and domestic.

Having noticed one of the enemy's armed vessels frequently passing across the Sound, and taking her station at anchor under Stratford Point, and learning that her special business was to bring over goods, and take back produce in return, as well as to annoy our commerce from East to West through the Sound, I began to entertain hopes that we might capture or destroy her. To this end, I rode over to Bridgeport to find some suitable vessel for the purpose. Capt. Hubbel had the very thing I wanted, and moreover wished to have the Sound freed from such a nuisance, as he wished to prosecute his accustomed voyages to Boston, etc. We finally came to the following agreement, viz.: Capt. Hubbel engaged so to manage and navigate his vessel as that he would absolutely come in contact with the enemy's sloop-of-war; which being done, I engaged to take her or pay him for his vessel, which must of course fall into the enemy's hands. I accordingly ordered 45 men from my detachment, under the immediate orders of Lieuts. Rhea and Stanley, of the Legion, together with Capt. Brewster's boat's crew of continental troops, to be held ready for service. On the 20th of February, 1783, the same vessel was discovered under Stratford Point. The troops were immediately embarked—the whole to be commanded by Capt. Brewster—with particular orders not to appear on deck until they should be needed. Capt. Amos Hubbel, who commanded our vessel, left his anchorage at about 2 o'clock, and at 4 P. M. the vessels were within speaking distance. The enemy immediately commenced a full discharge of their cannon and swivels, which crippled Capt. Hubbel's vessel in her hull, mast, and rigging very considerably. He, however, stood at the helm himself, and although a shot had passed through his mast, yet he brought his *bow* directly across the *side* of the British ship.

When within a few yards of each other, the order was given for the troops to appear on deck, when the command to fire immediately followed, and in a moment the two vessels came in contact, when the whole detachment boarded the enemy's ship with fixed bayonets, and she was captured as in a moment. Nearly every man on board, was either killed or wounded, while not a man of our detachment was hurt.

In a few hours both vessels were snugly moored at Blackrock harbor, and all was again quiet. I reported this affair to the Comander-in-Chief, who returned his thanks in his letter dated February 26th, 1783, and gave an order of condemnation of the prize, the avails of which were duly distributed to the troops.

After this event we captured several boats, some belonging to the British and some to our side, for we served all that we found carrying on this illicit trade pretty much alike.

While I was prosecuting my military duties at the head of my brave detachment, after the campaign opened for the year 1783, on the 18th of April, the Commander-in-Chief announced in several orders the cessation of hostilities, as the preliminary articles of peace had been received by Congress. He therefore ordered the cessation of hostililites between the United States of America, and the King of Great Britain to be publicly proclaimed the next day at noon.

This seemed to put an end to the further effusion of blood. It was, however, by no means certain that peace would ensue, and the Commander-in-Chief called on me most pressingly to obtain information as to the probable movements of the enemy, as his letters will fully evince.

In the preceding month, when all seemed to suppose that peace was very near, an anonymous writer addressed the army in a style calculated to inflame their injured feelings, and to excite them to deeds of outrage and violence against their country.

The address was couched in language the most engaging, and calculated to inflame the angry passions of the army against that country for which they had fought and bled, and in whose cause they had sustained such unparalleled sufferings. The author of this anonymous address was then supposed to be Major Armstrong, who for some time had been an Aid-de-Camp to Gen. Gates. Within a little time past, Gen. Armstrong (then Major Armstrong) has acknowleged that he was the author of said anonymous address.

The Commander-in-Chief, having noticed and disapproved of said address in general orders, the next day a second anonymous paper made its appearance, more inflammatory, if possible, than the first. This induced Gen. Washington to convene the general and field officers of the army, with a deputation from the officers of the line, to whom he delivered a most interesting and feeling address, in which he wholly disapproved of the course proposed for the officers to pursue. He assured them that they might depend upon his exertions to obtain remuneration from the United States for their services, which he did not doubt would be done as soon as the Government could raise the money.

To this the officers responded most respectfully and affectionately, and assured their great leader and commander that they abhorred the measure proposed by the anonymous writer, and would not dishonor themselves by adopting the course by him suggested. This put a most fortunate end to this parricidal advice.

In view of the dissolution of the army, when the officers

would disperse, most probably never to meet again in this world, a proposal was made to establish a society to which every officer might belong, by subscribing to its principles. A committee having been appointed at the suggestion of Gen. Knox, and by the approbation of the Commander-in-Chief, to devise some suitable mode in which this object could be answered, and the mutual friendships of the officers of the army of the revolution maintained and cemented, a plan was drawn up and reported. On the 10th of May, 1783, the officers held their first meeting, at which the Baron Steuben, as senior officer, presided. Gens. Knox, Huntington, and Hand, with Capt. Shaw, were chosen a committee to revise the proposal which had been submitted as the basis of the Institution. On the 13th of the same month, another meeting was held at Baron Steuben's quarters, when the committee aforesaid reported a plan for establising a society, which was accepted, and is as follows :

"It has pleased the Supreme Governor of the Universe, in the disposition of human affairs, to cause the separation of the Colonies of North America from the domination of Great Britain, and after a bloody conflict of eight years, to establish them free, independent, and soverign States, connected by alliances founded on reciprocal advantages, with some of the greatest princes and powers of the earth.

" To perpetuate, therefore, as well the remembrance of this vast event, as the mutual friendships which have been formed under the pressure of common danger, and in many instances cemented by the blood of the parties, the officers of the American army do hereby in the most solemn manner associate, constitute, and combine themselves into one society of friends, to endure as long as they shall endure, or any of their eldest male posterity, and in failure thereof, the collateral branches, who may be judged worthy of becoming its supporters and members.

" The officers of the American army having generally been taken from the citizens of America, possess high veneration for the character of that illustrious Roman, Lucius Quintius Cincinnatus, and being resolved to follow his example, by returning to their citizenship, they think they may with propriety denominate themselves the Society of the Cincinnati.

"The following principles shall be immutable, and form the basis of the Society of the Cincinnati:

"An incessant attention to preserve inviolate those exalted rights and liberties of human nature for which they have fought and bled, and without which the high rank of a rational being is a curse instead of a blessing.

"An unalterable determination to promote and cherish between the respective States, that union and national honor so essentially necessary to their happiness and the future dignity of the American Confederacy.

"To render permanent the cordial affection subsisting among the officers, this spirit will dictate brotherly kindness in all things, and particularly extend to the most substantial acts of beneficence, according to the ability of the Society, towards those officers and their families who, unfortunately, may be under the necessity of receiving it.

"The General Society will, for the sake of frequent communication, be divided into State Societies, and those again into such districts as shall be directed by the State Society.

"The Societies of the districts to meet as often as shall be agreed on by the State Society. Those of the State, on the fourth of July annually, or oftener, if they shall find it expedient, and the General Society on the first Monday in May, annually, so long as they shall deem it necessary; afterwards at least once in every three years.

"At each meeting, the principles of the Institution will be fully considered, and the best measures to promote them adopted.

"The State Societies to have a President, Vice-President, Secretary, Treasurer, and Assistant Treasurer, to be chosen annually by a majority of votes at the State meeting.

"In order to form funds which may be respectable and assist the unfortunate, each officer shall deliver to the Treasurer of the State Society one month's pay, which shall remain forever to the use of the State Society, the interest only of which, if necessary, to be appropriated to the relief of the unfortunate.

"The Society shall have an order, by which its members shall be known and distinguished, which shall be a *medal of gold*, of a proper size to receive the emblems, and be suspended by a deep blue ribbon, two inches wide, edged with white, descriptive of the union of America and Fame."

Gen. Washington was chosen President of the General Society, and the officers in the respective States organized their State Societies. In the Connecticut line, to which I belonged, the officers generally deposited a month's pay in public securities, which, being afterwards funded by the government, made a handsome capital.

Being chosen Treasurer, I brought the capital stock to be a productive fund—the surplus interest being made a principal. In this office I continued several years, until I was chosen President of the Society, when I resigned the Treasurer's seals. In many of the States, acts of incorporation had been obtained for their State Societies, which became necessary for the protection of their funds. Application was made repeatedly for a like privilege for our State Society; but there seemed to be a jealousy in the minds of some that it would be like encouraging a sort of *self-erected aristocracy*.

About this time Gen. Washington, our President-General, feeling unwilling to do anything to excite a popular ferment, especially towards the officers of the late revolutionary army, proposed to the State Societies to abolish the Institution. He felt so unwilling to be instrumental in any way to such an end, that he requested Col. Humphreys to attend one of our anniversary meetings, and to explain his views and wishes to us. Having no prospect of obtaining a charter from the State to protect our funds, we discussed the subject pretty fully, and finally agreed to abolish the Institution in Connecticut. We further agreed to pass our funds over into the hands of the Treasurer of Yale College, leaving it optional with every officer to withdraw his subscription, or not, as he pleased.

Peace having finally been agreed on between Great Britain and the United States of America, on the second of September, 1783. Gen. Washington issued his farewell orders to the armies of the United States, which he had commanded for the previous eight years. His language was so impressive, and his advice so appropriate, that I cannot deny myself the pleasure of transcribing them into my journal. Having taken notice of the proclamation of Congress under date of October 18th, 1783, he adds :

" It only remains for the Commander-in-Chief to address himself once more, and that for the last time, to the armies of the United States, however widely dispersed the individuals who composed them may be, and to bid them an affectionate, a long farewell. But before the Commander-in-Chief takes his final leave of those he holds most dear, he wishes to indulge himself a few moments in a brief review of the past.

" He will then take the liberty of exploring, with his military friends, their future prospects ; of advising the general line of conduct which, in his opinion, ought to be pursued, and he will conclude the address by expressing the obligations he feels himself under for the spirited and able assistance he has experienced from them in the performance of an arduous office.

" A contemplation of the complete attainment, at a period earlier than could have been expected, of the object for which we contended against so formidable a power, cannot but inspire us with astonishment and gratitude. The disadvantageous circumstances on our part with which the war was undertaken, can never be forgotten. The singular interpositions of Providence, in our feeble condition, were such as could scarcely escape the attention of the most unobserving. While the unparalleled perseverence of the armies of the United States, through almost every possible suffering and discouragement, for the space of eight long years, was little short of a standing miracle.

" It is not the meaning, nor within the compass of this address to detail the hardships peculiarly incident to our service, nor to describe the distresses which, in several instances, have resulted from the extremes of hunger and nakedness, combined with the rigors of an inclement season ; nor is it necessary to dwell on the dark side of our past affairs. Every American officer and soldier must now console himself for any unpleasant circumstances which may have occurred, by the recollection of the uncommon scenes in which he has been called to act no inglorious part, and the astonishing events of which he has been a witness—events which have seldom if ever before taken place on the stage of human action; nor can this probably ever happen again. For who has ever before seen a disciplined army formed from such raw materials? Who that was not a witness could imagine that the most violent local prejudices would cease so soon, and that men who came from the different parts of the continent, strongly disposed by the habits of education to despise and quarrel with each other, would instantly become one patriotic band of brothers? Or who that was not on the spot, can trace the steps by which such a wonderful revolution has been effected, and such a glorious period put to all our toils?

" It is universally acknowledged that the enlarged prospects of happiness, opened by the confirmation of our independence and sovereignty, almost exceed the power of description; and shall not the brave men who have contributed so essentially to those inestimable acquisitions, retiring victorious from the field of war to the field of agriculture, participate in all the blessings that have been obtained? In such a republic, who will exclude them from the rights of citizens, and the fruits of their labors?

" In such a country, so happily circumstanced, the pursuits of commerce and the cultivation of the soil will unfold to industry the certain road to competence. To those hardy soldiers who are actuated by the spirit of adventure, the fisheries will afford ample and profitable employment, and the extensive and fertile regions of the West will yield a most happy asylum to those who are fond of domestic employment, and seeking personal independence. Nor is it possible to conceive that any one of the United States will prefer a national bankruptcy and the dissolution of the Union, to a compliance with the requisitions of Congress, and the payment of its just debts, so that the officers and soldiers may expect considerable assistance in recommencing their civil occupations, from the sums due to them from the public, which must and will inevitably be paid.

" In order to effect this desirable purpose, and to remove the prejudices which may have taken possession of the minds of the good people of the States, it was earnestly recommended to all the troops, that with strong attachments to the Union, they should carry with them into civil society the most conciliatory dispositions, and that they should prove themselves not less virtuous and useful a citizens, than they have been persevering and victorious as soldiers. What though there should be some envious individuals, who are unwilling to pay the debt the public has contracted, or to yield the tribute due to merit; yet, let such unworthy treatment produce no invective, or any instance of intemperate conduct. Let it be remembered that the unbiased voice of the free citizens of the United States has promised the just reward, and given the merited applause. Let it be known and remembered that the reputation of the federal armies is established beyond the reach of malevolence, and let a consciousness of their achievements and fame still excite the men who composed them to honorable action, under the persuasion that the private virtues of economy, prudence, and industry, will not be less amiable in civil life, than the more splendid qualities of valor, perseverance, and enterprise were in the field. Every one may rest assured, that much of the future happiness of the officers and men will depend upon the wise and manly conduct which shall be adopted by them, when they are mingled with the great body of the community. And although the General has so frequently given it as his opinion, in the most public and explicit manner, that unless the principles of the federal government were properly supported, and the powers of the Union increased, the honor, dignity, and justice of the nation would be lost forever, yet he cannot help repeating on this occasion so interesting a sentiment, and leaving it as his last injunction to every officer and every soldier who may view the subject in the same serious point of light, to add his best endeavors to those of his worthy fellow-citizens towards effecting these great and valuable purposes on which our very existence as a nation so materially depends.

"The Commander-in-Chief conceives little now wanting to enable the soldier to change the military character into that of a citizen, but that steady, decent tenor of behavior, which has generally distinguished not only the army under his immediate command, but the different detachments and separate armies, through the course of the war. From their good sense and prudence, he anticipated the happiest results, and while he congratulates them on the glorious occasion which renders their services in the field no longer necessary, he wishes to express the strong obligations he feels himself under for the assistance he has received from every class, and in every instance where it was required. He presents his thanks in the most serious and affectionate manner to the general officers, as well for their counsel, on many interesting occasions, as for their ardor in promoting the success of the plans he has adopted ; to the commandants of regiments and corps, and to the officers, for their zeal and attention in carrying his orders promptly into execution ; to the staff, for their alacrity and exactness in performing the duties of their several departments ; and to the non-commissioned officers, and private soldiers, for their extraordinary patience in suffering, as well as their invincible fortitude in action. To all the branches of the army, the General takes this last and solemn opportunity of professing his inviolable attachment and friendship. He wishes more than bare professions were in his power, and that he was really able to be useful to them in future life. He flatters himself, however, they will do him the justice to believe, that whatever could with propriety be attempted by him, has been done. And being now about to conclude these his last public orders, to take his ultimate leave, in a short time, of the military character, and to bid a final adieu to the armies he has so long had the honor to command, he can only again offer, in their behalf, his recommendations to their grateful country, and his prayers to the God of America. May ample justice be done them here, and may the choicest of Heaven's favors, both here and hereafter, attend those who, under the divine auspices, have secured innumerable blessings for others. With these wishes, and this benediction, the Commander-in-Chief is about to retire from service. The curtain of separation will soon be drawn, and the military scene to him will be closed forever."

These were the closing general orders, issued to the armies of the United States, at the close of a war of *eight years' con-*

tinuance, prosecuted for the most glorious object for which freemen contend, attended with more appalling hardships and sufferings than have heretofore been borne by any body of military men ; sustained with more firmness and perseverance than history accords to any other army, and finally terminating in the complete attainment of the glorious prize for which they contended, viz., the *Independence of the United States of America*. No language can express the feelings of the army when the foregoing general orders were read. The most hardy soldiers were unable to restrain the copious flood of tears ; and to some of us, who had been honored with peculiar tokens of confidence and favor, the scene was absolutely overwhelming. For myself, the thought of being separated from my General, whom I loved with filial affection, and obeyed with perfect readiness and delight, was heart-rending in the extreme. The scene is quite vivid to my recollection now, more than *forty-five years* since it took place. No change of situation, no engagements in business, nor any new friendships have ever been permitted to abate that high regard, that profound respect, that ardor of affection, and that entire devotion of all my powers to the views and wishes of this illustrious man. I loved and venerated him through life, I most severely lamented his sudden and untimely death, and should greatly rejoice to be able to imitate, in some humble degree, his great example.

Before I close the scenes of my military life, I must revert to the Summer of 1783, after the preliminary articles of peace had been announced. As little doubt could be entertained but that peace would soon follow, I found it necessary to take some steps to insure the safety of several persons within the enemy's lines, who had served us faithfully and with intelligence during the war. As some of these were considered to be of the *Tory character*, who would be very obnoxious when the British army should depart, I suggested to Gen. Washington the propriety of my being permitted to go to New York, under the cover of a flag. This he very readily granted, and I proceeded to New York, where I was surrounded by British troops, tories, cowboys, and traitors. By the officers of the army and navy

I was treated with great respect and attention, and especially by the Commander-in-Chief, Gen. Carlton, at whose table I dined with the commanding officers of the navy, and others of high distinction. It was not a little amusing, to see how men, tories and refugees, who a little before uttered nothing but the terms, *rebels and traitors to their King*, against all the officers of the American army, would now come around me while in New York, and beg my protection against the dreaded rage of their countrymen. But I knew them too well too make any promises.

While at New York, I saw and secured all who had been friendly to us through the war, and especially our emissaries, so that not one instance occurred of any abuse, after we took possession of the city, where protection was given or engaged.

Having accomplished all my business in New York, I return-ed again to the army, and made my report to the Commander-in-Chief. The troops now began to be impatient to return to their respective homes, and those that were destined for that purpose, to take possession of the city. Gen. Washington now dismissed the greater part of the army in so judicious a way, that no unpleasant circumstances occurred. The 25th of November, 1783, was appointed for the British troops to evac-uate the city, and for the American troops to take possession of it. Gen. Knox, at the head of a select corps of American troops, entered the city as the rear of the British troops em-barked ; soon after which the Commander-in-Chief, accompa-nied by Gov. Clinton and their respective suites, made their pub-lic entry into the city on horseback, followed by the Lieut.-Gov-ernor and members of the Council. The officers of the army, eight abreast, and citizens on horseback, eight abreast, accompanied by the Speaker of the Assembly, and citizens on foot eight abreast, followed after the Commander-in-Chief and Gov. Clin-ton. So perfect was the order of march, that entire tranquil-ity prevailed, and nothing occurred to mar the general joy. Every countenance seemed to express the triumph of repub-lican principles over the military despotism which had so long pervaded this now happy city. Most of the refugees had em-barked for Nova Scotia, and the few who remained, were too insignificant to be noticed in the crowd. It was indeed a joyful day to the officers and soldiers of our army, and to all the friends of American independence, while the troops of the enemy, still in our waters, and the host of tories and refugees, were sorely mortified. The joy of meeting friends, who had long been separated by the cruel rigors of war, cannot be described.

Governor Clinton gave a public dinner, at which Gen. Washington and the principal officers of the army, citizens, etc., were present. On the Tuesday evening following, there was a most splendid display of fire-works, at the lower part of Broadway, near the Bowling Green. It far exceeded anything I had ever seen in my life.

The time now drew near when the Commander-in-Chief intended to leave this part of the country for his beloved retreat at Mount Vernon. On Tuesday, the 4th of December, it was made known to the officers then in New York, that Gen. Washington intended to commence his journey on that day. At 12 o'clock the officers repaired to *Francis' Tavern*, in Pearl Street, where Gen. Washington had appointed to meet them, and to take his final leave of them. We had been assembled but a few moments, when His Excellency entered the room. His emotion, too strong to be concealed, seemed to be reciprocated by every officer present. After partaking of a slight refreshment, in almost breathless silence, the General filled his glass with wine, and turning to the officers, he said: " With a heart full of love and gratitude, I now take leave of you. I most devoutly wish that your latter days may be as prosperous and happy as your former ones have been glorious and honorable."

After the officers had taken a glass of wine, Gen. Washington said: " I cannot come to each of you, but shall feel obliged if each of you will come and take me by the hand."

Gen. Knox being nearest to him, turned to the Commander-in Chief, who, suffused in tears, was incapable of utterance, but grasped his hand ; when they embraced each other in silence. In the same affectionate manner, every officer in the room marched up to, kissed, and parted with his General-in-Chief.

Such a scene of sorrow and weeping I had never before witnessed, and hope I may never be called upon to witness again. It was indeed too affecting to be of long continuance—for tears of deep sensibility filled every eye—and the heart seemed so full, that it was ready to burst from its wonted abode. Not a word was uttered to break the solemn silence that prevailed, or to interrupt the tenderness of the interesting scene. The *simple thought* that we were then about to part from the man who had conducted us through a long and bloody war, and under whose conduct the glory and independence of our country had been achieved, and that we should see his face no more in this world, seemed to me utterly insupportable. But the time of separation had come, and waiving his hand to his *grieving children* around him, he left the room, and passing through a corps of light infantry who were paraded to receive him, he walked silently on to Whitehall, where a barge was in waiting. We all followed in mournful silence to the wharf, where a prodigious crowd had assembled to witness the departure of the man who, under God, had been the great agent in establishing the glory and independence of these United States. As soon as he was seated, the barge put off into the river, and when out in the stream, our great and beloved General waived his hat, and bid us a silent adieu.

We paid him the same affectionate compliment, and then returned to the same hotel whence Gen. Washington had so recently departed. Thus closed one of the most interesting and affecting scenes that I ever witnessed—a scene so fraught with feeling, that it seemed for a time as if it never could be erased from vivid and constant reflection. But, such is the wise constitution of human nature, that other objects and pursuits occupy the mind and engross the attention, or life would become a burden too heavy to bear.

In a few days, all the officers who had assembled at New York to participate in the foregoing heart-rending scene, departed to their several places of abode, to commence anew their avocations for life.

Having for seven years been *banished from the home of my father*, at Brookhaven, in Suffolk county, on Long Island, I determined to visit the place of my nativity. Accordingly, I set out to pay my respects to my honored father and friends at Brookhaven aforesaid. Being principally Whigs, and now emancipated from their late severe bondage, the people had determined that they would celebrate the occasion by some public demonstration of their joy. They therefore concluded to have public notice given, that on a day near at hand, they would have an *ox roasted whole* on the public green, to partake of which all were invited to attend. I remember well, that after a most joyful meeting with my former friends (many of whom I had not seen since the war commenced), I was appointed master of ceremonies for the occasion. When the ox was well roasted, the noble animal on his spit was removed to a proper place, and after a blessing from the God of Battles had been invoked by my honored father, I began to carve, dissect, and distribute to the multitude around me. The aged and the young, the male and the female, rejoiced to receive a portion, which, from the novelty of the scene, and being in commemoration of so great an event, obtained a peculiar zest. All was harmony and joy, for all seemed to be of one mind.

A *Tory* could not have lived in that atmosphere one minute. By sunset the whole concourse—a vast multitude—dispersed and returned to their own homes in quietness and peace. The joy of the Whig population through the island was literally unbounded, nor could it be expected that their Tory neighbors would escape, unnoticed, through such a scene of rejoicing after victory. In some instances private satisfaction was taken in a pretty summary manner, but in most cases the milder process of law was resorted to and maintained.

From this most pleasing scene of liberality and public rejoicing, I concluded to take a ride quite to the East end of Long Island, Suffolk county, which embraces much the greatest part of Long Island, and had been well known to be friendly to the American cause. For this they had suffered much from the British troops, as well as from their adherents. In my journey down the island, my reception by the inhabitants was most gratifying. Private hospitality and public honor were most liberally bestowed on any man who had served in the revolutionary army.

The Autumn and Winter of 1783 were devoted very much to these most pleasing and delightful visitations. Among others (not the least pleasant and interesting) were those which secured to me a *companion and friend*, the most desirable, in my view, had I been privileged with a choice from her whole sex. After visiting Connecticut, and arranging and settling my plans for mercantile life, in the place where I now reside, on the 18th of March, 1784, I led Miss Floyd to the hymenial altar, and commenced the life and duties of a married man. She was the eldest daughter of the Hon. William Floyd, of Mastic, Long Island. He was a man of very extensive landed possessions on the island, but having actively engaged on the side and in the cause of his country, he was obliged to abandon his estates, and was a member of Congress through the war. As soon as peace was proclaimed, he, with many others who had left their property in the hands or under the control of the common enemy, returned to their homes. These they found, for the most part, sadly changed for the worse. But it was very comforting to all who had suffered . this voluntary banishment from their own soil, once more to place the soles of their feet upon it. The nuptials of Miss Floyd and myself were solemnized on the 18th of March, 1784, my honored father officiating, when Gen. Floyd gave a most sumptuous entertainment to a great number of invited guests.

Soon after our marriage, we paid a visit to New York, where we found a great number of friends, with whom we spent a few weeks very pleasantly. We were treated with great hospitality by the family of Mr. Joseph Hallett, at whose hospitable abode we were invited to take up our lodgings. After this visit was ended, we returned back to Mastic, calling on our friends on the North side of Long Island and on Shelter Island, whom we wished to see before we departed to our abode at Litchfield, Connecticut. We took a jaunt down the island, which was considered rather as a parting visit. In this also we had a very pleasant journey, and time seemed to glide insensibly away, which brought us every day nearer to the period when we expected to bid Long Island a final adieu as our home. Indeed, I had not made it my place of residence since I entered college in the year 1769, and as for my beloved partner, she had never seen her father's house since the family left it in the year 1776, when the British troops took possession of it and New York.

1784. Having now closed the scenes of my military life with the past year, which had been of almost eight years' continuance, and being about to commence an entirely new pursuit, most probably for life, a few reflections very naturally arise in my mind, in reviewing the subject. In the first place, the contemplation of the momentous events of the revolutionary war, in which I had taken some humble part, fills my mind with wonder and astonishment. When I reflect on the condition of these colonies when the battles of *Lexington* and *Bunker Hill* were fought, and the first hostile gun was fired, compared with that of Great Britain—our enemy—it looks almost like madness to have ventured on the mighty conflict, and little less than a miracle that we were sustained through such a bloody war, and finally came out of it completely victorious. 2nd. When I reflect upon the hardships and dangers to which I was exposed in such a conflict, and the very peculiar hazards which befell me at times in the execution of duties which devolved upon me, aside from those that are common to a military life, I can scarcely credit my recollections on this subject. But when I further reflect that, in all the general battles that were fought, when the 2nd Regiment of Light Dragoons took a part, I never failed to be at the head of my corps, and more especially that in many *separate enterprises* in which I was engaged, and in which I had the sole responsibility and command, attended with peculiar dangers, both on the land and by water, and that through the whole my life has not only been preserved, but I have never received a *dangerous wound*, nor had a *single bone broken*, I seem to myself a singular instance of the Divine protection and care.

In this review of the special mercies of God vouchsafed to me, I desire most devoutly to adore and bless His protecting hand, and call on my soul and every faculty that I possess to adore and praise my Divine Benefactor.

3rd. In addition to the protection of a merciful Providence, I would notice the peculiar marks of attention which I uniformly received from the Commander-in-Chief through the war. Having been early and personally acquainted with this great man, I held him in high veneration, and when he appointed me, or rather requested me to take charge of *a particular part of his private correspondence*, this brought us into frequent and intimate correspondence. His approbation of my conduct, on many occasions, expressed both *publicly* and *privately* by letter, together with the favorable expression of Congress, afforded me the highest satisfaction that a soldier could receive.

4th. Among all the vices and false pursuits to which the military life is liable, perhaps none is more prominent than *dueling*. Having early imbibed the sentiment, that no man had a right to expose his life in this manner, I openly avowed my opinion, and yet amidst all the clashing of interests and opinions to which we were exposed, I never was called upon to defend my honor by this heaven-daring resort.

I always determined that I never would be guilty of this *murderous sin*, and yet I am not conscious that any man ever thought me to be a coward. For this early imbibed opinion and subsequent restraining conduct, I desire most humbly and devoutly to adore and bless God.

BENJAMIN TALLMADGE.

REMARKS.

The foregoing memoir was prepared by my venerable parent, and I will briefly add, that Col. Tallmadge continued to reside in Litchfield, Connecticut, until his death, which occurred on the 7th of March, 1835 ; having lost my mother on the 3rd of June, 1805, leaving five sons and two daughters.

On the 3rd of May, 1808, he married the daughter of Joseph Hallett, Esq., of the city of New York, who survived him but a few years.

Col. Tallmadge, after the close of the revolution, engaged extensively in commercial pursuits in Litchfield, Connecticut, and elsewhere. In 1800, he was elected a Representative in Congress from the State of Connecticut, and was continued by successive elections as such Representative, until 1816, when he declined a further election. In 1812, he was tendered by President Madison a high and prominent command in the Northern division of the army of the United States, which he declined.

At the formation of the Society of the Cincinnati for the State of Connecticut, he was elected their Treasurer and then President, and continued as such until their dissolution.

After leaving Congress, Col. Tallmadge was appointed the President of a Banking Institution at Litchfield, which, with his domestic duties, afforded him sufficient occupation for his declining years. He died at the mature age of 82 years, crowned by all the temporal honors that the most ambitious could covet, and, as we trust, realizing on his separation from life, that higher crown of glory which seemed to be the highest ambition of his well-spent life.

During his long official life, he became associated with most of the distinguished men of our country, and enjoyed the respect and confidence of the Quincys, the Pickerings, the Trumbulls, the Morrises, the Rutledges, the Griswolds, and the Bayards of that day.

It was a source of great pleasure to Col. Tallmadge to meet with the companions of his revolutionary struggles, and many now recollect the interesting and affectionate interview that occurred between himself and Lafayette, at New Haven, on his late visit to this country after so many years of separation. They embraced and wept at the interview when they recurred to the trying scenes through which they had passed in the ardency of youth, and that they were severally blessed by the grateful feelings of their countrymen, and the most distinguished notice of our government.

F. A. TALLMADGE.

CPSIA information can be obtained at www.ICGtesting.com
Printed in the USA
LVOW04s0420040315

429196LV00027B/628/P